SAVING THE
DEAL

SAVING THE
DEAL

How to Avoid Financing Fiascoes and Other Real Estate Deal Killers

Tracey Rumsey

AMACOM

American Management Association

New York • Atlanta • Brussels • Chicago • Mexico City • San Francisco
Shanghai • Tokyo • Toronto • Washington, D.C.

Special discounts on bulk quantities of AMACOM books are
available to corporations, professional associations, and other
organizations. For details, contact Special Sales Department,
AMACOM, a division of American Management Association,
1601 Broadway, New York, NY 10019.
Tel.: 212-903-8316 Fax: 212-903-8083
E-mail: specialsls@amanet.org
Website: www.amacombooks.org/go/specialsales
To view all AMACOM titles go to: www.amacombooks.org

This publication is designed to provide accurate and authoritative
information in regard to the subject matter covered. It is sold with the
understanding that the publisher is not engaged in rendering legal,
accounting, or other professional service. If legal advice or other expert
assistance is required, the services of a competent professional person
should be sought.

REALTOR® is a registered collective membership mark that identifies a
real estate professional who is a member of the National Association of
REALTORS® and subscribes to its strict Code of Ethics. AMACOM uses
this term throughout this book in initial capital letters or ALL CAPITAL
letters for editorial purposes only, with no intention of trademark
violation.

Library of Congress Cataloging-in-Publication Data

Rumsey, Tracey.
    Saving the deal : how to avoid financing fiascoes and other real estate deal killers /
Tracey Rumsey.
      p. cm.
    Includes bibliographical references and index.
    ISBN-13: 978-0-8144-0030-2
    ISBN-10: 0-8144-0030-2
    1. Mortgage loans—United States.   2. House buying—United States.   3. Real estate
business—United States.   I. Title.

HG2040.5.U5R86   2008
333.33′80688—dc22
                                                                                            200703312

Printing Number

10   9   8   7   6   5   4   3   2   1

Contents

CONTENTS

Introduction

Lessons learned the hard way: All of us have them, and Realtors are certainly no exception. Sometimes the deal died. Sometimes it was only delayed. But the negative situation left in its wake disappointed clients and wasted time. Not only are these lessons painful and sometimes embarrassing, but in the real estate world, they are costly. *The buck stops here* takes on a whole new literal meaning when your sale blows up two days before settlement!

As a mortgage loan officer, I have seen firsthand all too many ways a deal can fall apart. So it seemed to me that someone should keep track of all these things that can ruin a deal, as well as the things that you, as a Realtor, can do to save the deal. My idea was to write them down and pass them on to other agents so that the same mistakes aren't repeated again and again.

The best news of all is that clients will love you when you've got all this information at your fingertips. You can answer their questions and provide them with valuable advice during every stage of the deal. You'll be able to warn of potential problems before they result in a disaster down the road. Remember that, in many instances, this is the first time they are buying or selling a home. But even if that's not the case, it's not something they do every day, so being able to guide them through the process will make you their hero—and probably turn them into a repeat client down the road.

The Realtor education starts with the pre-licensing phase. Educators teach you to pass a test. Your focus is contracts, law, and the language of real estate. You then find a job with a brokerage that promises to mentor and train you into a successful agent. Now you are in the never-ending marketing stage of your new business. Phone calls, door hangers, mailers, relationship building: You are doing it all. Or maybe you are starting as an assistant to someone else. Whatever the path, it's at this stage of your career that your license and dazzling personality aren't enough. You've got to bring something extra to the dance.

You will be advised to "build a team" to support your fledgling business. This is a critical part of your success, I agree. So you go out to gather your lenders, title companies, home inspectors, etc. that will make up your trusted panel of professionals. You've lined up an A1 list of the best-of-the-best in your area. Giddy with the expertise firepower this group of gurus provides, you can hardly wait for the next client to appear.

But you're making a big mistake if you simply decide that your job is to market, market, market and you'll let everyone else do their job, never bothering to understand what it is they do. Unless you have the luxury of working in cash transactions, the world of mortgage and title will make or break every deal. And the more you know about these areas, the better.

Education and proactive thinking are the keys to "leading" your transactions instead of huddling in the corner with your fingers crossed. Prepare yourself to wow the client by being ready for those frontline questions that will be fired at you upon your first contact with a buyer or seller. In a perfect world, a buyer comes to you fully pre-approved and a seller aware of his or her property's title status. Your reality is that on a Saturday afternoon, a buyer walks into your open house with more questions about mortgage qualifying than about the house you are showing, and many sellers are listing while in crisis mode due to death or divorce.

So in this proactive education spirit, I started compiling notes during staff meetings and chats with underwriters, Realtors, escrow officers, and other loan officers. I'd overhear a horror story about a closing that happened (or didn't happen) and think, *Geez! Somebody should write that down! Somebody should tell somebody!* As a continuing education instructor, my classes were ripe with real estate agents and loan officers sharing their nightmare scenarios. As a loan officer, new clients would come to me in tears after their loan fell apart with another lender. Of course, they needed a new loan and speedy settlement or they will lose the house of their dreams. Some experiences were unique, but frequently the problems were the same. Hence, more proof that somebody should do something!

For the next five years I listened, I interviewed people, and I wrote down what I heard. I can now offer you this ounce of prevention to avoid the painful pound of cure too many have experienced. Every Realtor accumulates a diverse set of experiences. Every deal is different. Every buyer and seller defines what you have to offer. My goal is to ramp up your knowledge base in a short amount of time with no pain at all! No delayed transactions. No dead deals. No lost commissions. I want you to be the forward-thinking hero who safely guides your transaction through the mortgage and title mine field and on to a triumphant settlement! (Tights and cape are optional.)

P.S. During the writing of this book we have seen an unprecedented change in the mortgage industry. The changes to or elimination of many types of loan products is forcing lenders and Realtors to work again within the parameters of conventional, FHA, VA, and state housing lending. In other words, it's back to the basics.

This book will provide a great refresher to those veteran agents who have gotten rusty on these products, and it can help newer agents get up to speed faster as they work tirelessly to get each transaction to settlement. I believe your future success at moving your listings and representing qualified buyers will be directly tied to your knowledge of these loan types.

Because my entire career has been centered around this type of lending, several chapters are specifically dedicated to these very products. Good news for you, since this will be the lending environment you have to navigate in for the foreseeable future. Read on, learn much, and laugh when you can. We're all in for a bumpy ride.

SAVING THE
DEAL

CHAPTER 1

Smoothing Out Title Tangles

Real estate title: It's the evidence of legal ownership of the property you are trying to help your client sell or buy. Somebody owns the house. Somebody wants to buy the house. Sign a deed. Record a deed. Seems like a pretty simple description of the entire transaction, right?

Now insert variables like death, divorce, bankruptcy, and war. Add in multiple owners under various legal entities. Suddenly it's not so simple anymore.

The following examples will give you some perspective on problem solving many issues right from the start and avoiding the dreaded last-minute mayhem that can descend on your deal.

DIVORCE DILEMMA

It's a glorious day! You just listed a home, the golden goose of the real estate sales world. You're excited! Your sales presentation was sharp. You researched the comparable sales in the neighborhood. Jake and Rhonda Miller are such a cute couple. You gave them fabulous, inexpensive staging tips to help the home show better. They loved you. They listed with you. Are you good or what?

Fast forward ten days. Your listing is under contract and the Millers really love you now. You've helped them find the perfect new home and you are planning on concurrent settlements in three weeks. Your favorite title person (part of your über team) calls to ask if you know how to contact Rachel Miller.

"Who is Rachel Miller?" you ask.

"The person holding title to your listing with Jake Miller," she replies. "Sorry I didn't ask sooner but the names were similar; you know, Rhonda and Rachel. My assistant just caught this today."

"Oops! Must be an ex-wife," you respond. "No problem. I'll call Jake and get some contact information. Funny, Jake never mentioned this when I met them to list the house. I'm sure it will be an easy fix since Jake wasn't concerned enough about it to say anything. I'll call you soon."

You call Jake.

"Hi, Jake. It's me, your Realtor Extrordinaire," you say. "Sorry to bother you at work but the title company just called to let me know that you are holding title with Rachel Miller, not Rhonda Miller. Can you fill me in?"

"Oh, sure," Jake answers. "Rachel is my ex-wife. We divorced three years ago. I was awarded the house in our divorce decree and we agreed on an equity buyout. I paid her and she signed a quit claim deed. It's all been taken care of. I thought everything had been done."

"Great!" you exclaim. "We just need to get that quit claim deed recorded at the county and we'll be back on track. Do you have it?"

"No. Rachel said she signed it and took it to the county. We weren't fighting about anything. I assumed she did it. We parted on good terms and we still stay in touch."

"Could one of the attorneys involved in the divorce have it?"

"We didn't use attorneys. We wanted to save the money so we filed ourselves with one of those forms we found online. This isn't going to be a problem, is it?" he asks, irritation creeping into his voice. "We've already turned in our change of address forms at the post office and scheduled the movers. Rhonda has already put a deposit down on new carpet for the family room."

"This shouldn't be a big deal, Jake," you answer, keeping your tone light but assured. "If you can just call Rachel, and get the original form from her, that will take care of things. Worst case, the title company can prepare a new quit claim deed and we'll have her sign it. Problem solved."

"Well, then, I guess we do have a problem," he says, angry now. "Rachel left last weekend for vacation. She—"

"Okay then," you interrupt, making sure to remain optimistic, "we'll just contact her at her hotel and have a new document sent to her there by FedEx. She can overnight it back." *Do not panic*, you think to yourself. *I'm in control. I'm the agent he loves. Keep him calm.*

"No, we can't," he says in exasperation. "She is backpacking in the Patagonia region of the Andes. For six weeks." Silence. He is awaiting your response.

"Oh," you reply. "Well . . ."

Patagonia, you think. *That sounds familiar. I should know where that is. Isn't that a clothing label? Do people really go there? Wherever it is, it doesn't sound like there's a FedEx drop. Oh my God, this isn't happening. Think! Plan C, I need a plan C!. Extensions: We'll get everybody to agree to a five- week extension. But what if they won't!? Ugh, why me?*

Now rewind to your first meeting with the Millers. They are still a cute couple. They still love you. The difference this time is that you've done your homework and you ask about the Rachel issue now, not later.

"I've looked at the county records and it shows the owners as Jake and Rachel Miller," you say. "Tell me about Rachel so we can plan for addressing this issue up front."

"That can't be right," Jake says. "That was supposed to be taken care of three years ago."

So you hear the story, and you outline the options for the Millers.

"Wow," Jake says. "I'm so glad you said something

today because I just ran into Rachel's mom in the grocery store and she told me Rachel is leaving next Friday and won't be back for six weeks. Some crazy backpacking trip in the Andes with tents and the whole bit. I had no idea this hadn't been done. You are the best!"

The lesson here is pretty straightforward: Never assume. Don't just ask a seller how they are holding title. Look it up. A little pre-meeting homework can prevent problems and really impress a potential client. Who's going to get the listing? The Realtor whose presentation was a little flashier than yours, or you, who walked in their door with a dragon in one hand and the sword to slay it in the other?

Many title companies offer access to a limited amount of county title information through their websites. Many counties are making information available online to the general public. For a small fee, some counties will give you an account with access to the actual abstract. You can print out documents recorded against that property. This instant access allows you to take that listing appointment at 4:00 p.m. today and still arrive prepared. In my opinion, it is well worth the money to have the information sooner as opposed to later.

Now let's look at some more common title status situations and how to deal with each one.

UNPAID CHILD SUPPORT

Unpaid child support can stop a settlement in its tracks, literally at the settlement table. An escrow officer told me about a seller who made a comment at settlement about his child support payments. The escrow officer asked him if he was current on those payments. He said no. Everything stopped right there. The escrow officer then had to follow up on this information, research with the child support enforcement agency any unpaid or overdue amounts, and collect them from the seller's proceeds. There were no judgments filed yet against the seller, but the escrow officer still had the obligation to protect the title of the property that her company was about to insure.

Avoid embarrassment and frustration for you and your client by asking this question before the escrow officer does. (See Appendix B: Home Listing Checklist for how to incorporate this and many more items discussed in this book as suggested questions for each new prospective seller.)

SELLER WHO CAN'T SELL, PART 1: THE WARRANTY DEED

Carol wants to sell her home. You discover at the listing appointment that Carol recently lost her husband, Bill, to cancer. This home holds too many painful memories and she wants to move on. She also tells you that this home was Bill's before they got married; Bill is her second husband.

This explanation helps the pieces fall into place. You don't want to repeat your experience with the Millers, so you check the county records that morning and notice that Carol does not hold title to the property she wants to sell. She goes on to tell you that Bill wanted her to have the home after he was gone, so he filled out a warranty deed that a local title company prepared and had her put it in their safe deposit box.

You explain to Carol that the warranty deed will need to be recorded at the county so that she can go forward with selling the house. You mention that your favorite title company can assist her with this process as part of the sale. She is grateful for your guidance. She knew something needed to be done but wasn't sure what to do next. She wants to complete the listing paperwork and go forward. Another listing. Another client loves you.

I can tell you that any attorney reading this over your shoulder probably has gone into cardiac arrest about now. Terms like "sleeper deed" (warranty deeds executed and then held without being recorded) and "validity" are being sputtered as well. I can also tell you that the above scenario, in some states, plays out without a hitch. In the real-life story of Carol (I was the lender for the buyer of Carol's home), things didn't work out so well. Here's what happened:

The warranty deed went to the title company, where it was reviewed and dropped into the file for recording. Unfortunately, it was forgotten. Two days before settlement, the title company attempted to record the document, which was rejected by the county due to improper execution (the deed had been filled out wrong). Carol couldn't continue with the sale because—you guessed it—she didn't own the house.

Now we were looking at a minimum of eight weeks for probate proceedings. My buyers didn't want to wait for eight more weeks. They had to cancel moving trucks, find a storage unit to move their belongings into, and find a place to live while they looked for a new home to buy. Anybody see a lawsuit in that picture anywhere?

Here are two things you can do that might be a better way to handle a seller like Carol and protect yourself from some ugly liability:

1. Don't take a listing until the seller actually owns the property, no matter how logical the explanation. Always beware of sleeper deeds.

2. Direct the seller or sellers to a title company, or better yet, to a real estate attorney to get documents recorded immediately or determine the necessary path to resolution.

In Carol's situation, the above steps certainly wouldn't have avoided probate, but they would have started the process sooner and prevented you from representing a home that couldn't be sold.

SELLER WHO CAN'T SELL, PART 2: THE GUARDIAN

Richard wants to sell his mother's home. Richard's mother is currently in a long-term care facility and her health is seriously deteriorating. Again, you did your homework and you know that Richard is not on title to this home. When you bring this up at the listing appointment, Richard produces guardianship papers and explains he is his mother's court-appointed guardian.

Everything seems official. We should be able to just provide these documents to the title company and go forward, right? Wrong. Your title company will tell you, as soon as you deliver these documents and the listing agreement, that your seller can't sell. Why? Because guardianship doesn't grant fiduciary power or the right to convey property. Conservatorship is required to carry out these matters for an individual. Richard needs to be named as conservator for his mother in order to proceed. Again, directing him to an attorney, sooner rather than later, can put this transaction on the right path.

SELLER WHO CAN'T SELL, PART 3: TENANTS IN COMMON

While working on this chapter, I have encountered yet another new example of a seller who can't sell. Just when I think I've seen it all, I have a new curve ball hurled at my head from the great real estate gods in the sky. (Do you see why I had to write this book? Once again, my pain is your gain, and this item will be added to your Home Offer/Buyer Checklist. This will be just one more reason your clients will love you and be loyal forever.)

I had the privilege of helping a young Ukrainian couple, Anya and Nikolai Zharov (names have been changed), purchase their first home in 2002. They were a joy to work with, as well as being an immigration success story. Attending that settlement and watching their 10-year-old daughter's face light up each time we talked about her new bedroom was definitely a highlight of my career.

Recently, I received a call from Anya. She needed my help. As she filled me in on the events of her life for the past five years, I discovered that Nikolai had died three years earlier in a car accident. Anya had since remarried and she and her new husband were considering selling the home and purchasing a new one. She wanted to discuss qualifying for a new mortgage, but her main concern was title-related. "How does this work when I sell the home?" she asked. "I still own the home with Nikolai."

I advised her that seeking legal counsel is always a good idea as I am not an attorney; however, I added, having title transferred solely into her name should not be difficult. Her Trust Deed (in Utah, we use Trust Deeds not Mortgages as our legal document) was prepared with the borrowers vested as "husband and wife as joint tenants." This implies full rights of survivorship. She should be able to go to the county, present Nikolai's death certificate, and that would be that. The county would record the death certificate and she would have sole ownership of the home.

The next day, Anya stopped by my office, frustrated and looking for more answers. When she went to the county and presented the death certificate, they looked up her property and informed her that she would have to get an attorney. They provided her a copy of the Warranty Deed that was signed by the seller conveying title to her and Nikolai and explained that the deed was the problem. She immediately brought it to me.

Here's what happened: The Warranty Deed, which is prepared by the title company for the seller to sign, (and should reflect the same verbiage as the Trust Deed) read "hereby convey and warrant to Anya Zharov and Nikolai Zharov"—and that was it. There was no vesting language whatsoever. The Warranty Deed is the document used to determine ownership, not my Trust Deed. The county doesn't care what my Trust Deed says. Because there is no specific vesting language, the ownership is treated as tenants in common. There are no rights of survivorship. She, Anya, will have to probate Nikolai's half of ownership in the home.

Of course, this saga will continue. The document was prepared in error and the borrower never approved it. There are liability issues here on the cost of probate, not to mention a title policy that was issued, etc. While I can't yet tell you how the story ends, I can convey this important three-part message:

1. Understand vesting language for your state.

2. Have the escrow officer/attorney explain the options to your client at closing to be sure that the client's wishes are carried out in the Warranty Deed.

3. At closing, request that you and your buyer see a copy of the Warranty Deed before it is recorded and verify the vesting language.

Put these tips into your tool box and use them at every buyer's closing. You can never have too many preventative measures when it comes to title issues.

Now, on to more title tangles.

THE "B" WORD

Bankruptcy can affect your seller's title depending on the type and status of the bankruptcy. In a later chapter, we'll look at bankruptcy's effect on a buyer's ability to get a mortgage, but bankruptcy can have consequences for sellers, too.

Because bankruptcy can be embarrassing for sellers, they may not volunteer the information. This is where the right questions up front can save everyone time and confusion down the road.

The two types of bankruptcy most commonly seen in conjunction with sellers are Chapter 7 and Chapter 13. Chapter 7 allows the debtor to have certain debts discharged, in most cases with no obligation of repayment. A Chapter 7 bankruptcy can be filed and completed in as little as four months in some states, with a final Discharge of Debtor signaling the completion of the process. Chapter 13 allows for debt adjustment and a three- to five-year repayment plan, with a trustee collecting and disbursing the funds to creditors. After the payment plan is complete, a Discharge of Debtor is issued.

Sellers who have completed a Chapter 7 bankruptcy are no longer personally liable for the discharged debts. However, any portion of that debt filed as a lien against their property is still valid. Escrow officers tell me they've seen some people go back to court and get the lien dismissed, but in most cases the lien stands. This may dramatically affect a seller's proceeds at closing, as the title company will have to collect funds to clear that lien. This is a little known fact and can be an unwelcome surprise at closing. Also, sellers currently involved in filing a Chapter 7 bankruptcy will need to complete the process, in most cases, before the home sale can go forward.

Chapter 13 works differently. With permission from the trustee, a seller is allowed to sell their home, buy a new one, or both during the re-payment process. A discharge is not necessary. In my professional experience, trustee permission has been about a one-week process. Getting this process rolling right away will get you to a successful settlement that much faster.

WHO IS THE SELLER?

Investors represent a much larger segment of the home buying/selling clientele than ever before. In recent years, a strong real estate market combined with new investor-friendly, low- or no-down mortgage products has made real estate investment easier and more attractive to all kinds of people and groups. Now throw in late-night infomercials and weekend seminars on getting rich in real estate and you end up with more kinds of entities holding title to real estate than you can shake a stick at.

So, you have a listing appointment and your title homework reveals that this home is owned by Four Brothers, LLC (limited liability company), ABC Family, Inc. (corporation), Jones Family Trust, or the Acme Partnership. Whatever the entity, there are two big questions looming on the horizon from your title company as soon as you turn in this contract and order title work:

1. Is this entity in good standing with the state?

2. Who is authorized to convey real property?

To answer these questions, a couple of things must happen. The title company will check with the state to verify that all filings and fees are up-to-date. If the entity is not in good standing, your client will be hustling to fix that. Many times corporations that haven't had much activity in past years get pulled out, dusted off, and used for the first time in awhile. Filings and fees get overlooked. A heads-up comment from you at the listing appointment will get things moving if this is a problem.

The next items to be checked will be a copy of the entity's Articles of Incorporation and Bylaws, Operating Agreement, etc. to determine who has the right to convey real estate. If individuals are not specified, then *all* of the partners/officers must sign. This can get a little crazy when the Acme Partnership is made up of six siblings, two of whom are not currently speaking to the others, four who live out of state, and one who has a trip to Europe planned during your scheduled closing date.

I don't mean to be overly dramatic, but I'm not making this stuff up. Seasoned veterans of the real estate industry can share these crazy stories all day long. Of course, the majority of your investor listings will go off without a hitch. It's that one deal a year that will give you the ulcers. Again, asking for documents up front, getting the proper signatures on your listing agreement, and advising clients of challenges early can keep a client returning year after year.

POWERS-OF-ATTORNEY

A power-of-attorney is a handy little item that can save a deal when one of the buyers or sellers cannot be present to sign documents. The simple question, "Will everyone be in town to sign on the day of settlement?" is an important one. Using a power-of-attorney has become especially common since September 11. Quite often, overseas deployment of military/National Guard members prevents a client from being present for a settlement.

The problem with using a power-of-attorney for a real estate transaction is that it must be a *specific* power-of-attorney that includes the property address and is used solely for the purpose of the transaction. It is typically drawn up by the escrow officer or attorney and then recorded at the county. A general power-of-attorney will not work.

Military families are always frustrated when this fact comes to light. It is standard that a deploying soldier will execute a general power-of-attorney for use by his or her spouse while they are gone. They assume that this is all they need.

Here's where you and your superior service come in. Once it's determined that a client won't be available to sign documents, you can start work on a game plan. Hopefully, the soon-to-depart signer is still around, so a power-of-attorney can be executed before they leave. Sometimes military members already deployed can be easily reached and sometimes they can't. Whatever the challenges, everyone appreciates the Realtor who provides this information at the first meeting rather than informing them weeks later that a problem exists.

BUYERS' AGENTS ALERT

In the introduction I mentioned leading your transaction. Leading means taking charge. The best offense is a good defense, etc. Call it leading, call it orchestrating. Call it babysitting, even—sometimes a more accurate description. The bottom line is, you have to do it or hire someone who will.

As the buyer's agent, you might think, "Title issues are not my concern. The selling agent has to worry about that." You're right. The selling agent should be on top of title issues. They should be detecting problems and working to rectify them before settlement, preferably before they ever took the listing.

However, the reality is you are always at the mercy of the expertise level of the other agent. Don't assume anything. Review the title carefully. Ask questions and demand answers. Deals can be saved by proactive thinking at the beginning of the transaction. Blowups or delays just before settlement, no matter who is at fault, hurt your client and your reputation. Your clients may logically understand that the problem had nothing to do with you, but there may still be negative emotions tied to you that may prevent them from calling in the future when they need an agent. Troubleshooting title issues early in a transaction will help you remain the agent that they love.

CHAPTER 2

Preparing Realistic Net Sheets

It's time for me to get up on my soapbox. Wouldn't you agree that when someone sells a home, the most important thing to the seller—outside of actually getting the home sold—is how much money they will walk away with? I sold my home last year and I know that it was the biggest concern I had. Yet I am astounded at how many agents and their brokers share the attitude: "Get the listing, get an offer, and then talk numbers." Why would you do this? I've heard, "Well, we do sketch out some basics at the listing appointment and then look at things in more detail when an offer comes in." Is your time not valuable? Can you afford to list a home that ultimately gets pulled from the market because the sellers can't afford to sell? Don't you want to retain your title of Realtor Extraordinaire and be the agent they love?

Net sheets are a great springboard to successful client relationships and closings. You want to start a listing appointment with the end in mind. If you want to set up realistic expectations in the beginning, guiding the seller through the numbers of that future final settlement statement is a must.

Let's say that you are a believer in the sketch-some-basics approach. At your listing appointment, you discuss sales price, current mortgage balances, and your 6% commission. You sell the clients on your experience, sales track record, and proven marketing plan for their home. They love you. They list with you.

The second you walk out their door, unless these are savvy sellers who clearly remember their last closing, they now expect that if they get a full price offer they will walk away with their sales price less their current mortgage balance and your 6% commission. That's what they're counting on. That's the number they keep using as they plan for down payment on a new home, moving costs, equity split with the ex, or whatever their expected final cash will be needed for.

Below is an example of a net sheet that will walk you and your client through all of the costs of selling a home. Aside from any needed property repairs or pre-listing cosmetic fixes, this sheet will offer a realistic look at estimated final numbers on closing day. Let's look at it line by line.

EQUITY WORKSHEET

☺ Projected Sales Price: $ _____

Less Selling Costs:

☹ 1st mortgage payoff	$ _____	(prin bal + 1 mo int)
☹ 2nd mortgage payoff	$ _____	(prin bal + 1 mo int)
☹ Mtg pre-payment penalties	$ _____	
☹ Sales comm ____%	$ _____	
☹ Title insurance for buyer	$ _____	
☹ Closing & recording fees	$ _____	
☹ Utility assessments	$ _____	
☹ Property tax pro ration	$ _____	
☹ Buyer's closing costs	$ _____	(if you agreed to pay)
☹ Home warranty	$ _____	(if you agreed to provide)
☹ Judgements/Debt payoffs	$ _____	
☹ Other _____	$ _____	

☹ Total Selling Costs: $ _____

☺ Estimated Proceeds From Sale (the bottom line): $ _____

FIRST MORTGAGE PAYOFF

If you ask your clients what they owe on their first mortgage, they will typically grab their last statement out of a drawer or jump online and quote you their current principal balance. In their mind, this is what they owe on this mortgage and therefore this number represents an accurate payoff. This is an understandable assumption, but it is not quite accurate.

The way it really works is that mortgage interest is paid in arrears. When you make your June 1 payment you are paying interest for the month of May. If you are selling your home on June 28 your payoff will be calculated as the June 1 principal balance (after your June 1 payment) plus interest for each day of June until the mortgage company receives the payoff. Hence my comment on this line: principal balance + one month's interest. This number will never be perfectly accurate, as we don't know exactly when the home will sell, how many additional payments will be made, etc. But with the size of today's mortgages, that one month's interest can be thousands of dollars. It has a major impact on the bottom line, so you don't want to leave it out.

SECOND MORTGAGE PAYOFF

This is the same story as the first mortgage payoff. The interest works the same way. However, some clients don't realize that the line of credit they took out at their local bank or credit union was tied to their home. I've seen this quite a few times in mortgage applications. As I review a credit report with the applicant, I will see a line item that says mortgage or home equity. Their response is, "That's not a mortgage. It's just a line of credit I have." I then get to share the good news that this was recorded as a debt against their home and will have to be paid off at closing when they sell.

This is just another reason why it's so vital that you review the title report thoroughly after listing a property or research the property online before the listing appointment. Clients don't always understand their own situation.

MORTGAGE PRE-PAYMENT PENALTIES

Mortgage pre-payment penalties are the new "gotcha" of the mortgage world. Sub-prime mortgages are rarely done without them and sub-prime mortgages are more prevalent than ever. (Another soapbox I'll get on later.) The kicker is that most of the time, your sellers have no idea that they even have a pre-payment penalty. Since the title company gets the payoff for the property, this ugly news may not come to light until either the title company notices it on the payoff and lets you or your client know, or worst case scenario, when you get to the closing table. Major unpleasantness!

Pre-payment penalties are common on sub-prime loans because they lower the initial interest rate during the first one to five years, depending on the program. The typical pre-payment penalty goes something like this: If during the first three years of the loan, the borrower pre-pays more than 20% of the principal balance, he must pay the equivalent of 6 months of interest on the amount paid in excess of 20%.

Here's an example: Your clients owe $200,000 on their first mortgage. Their current interest rate is 8.5%. They have to pay a penalty on 80% of the $200,000 or $160,000. $160,000 × 8.5% / 12 months = $1133.33 interest per month. $1133.33 × 6 months = $6800. Ouch! That's a big chunk out of their bottom line.

Second mortgages work differently. There are two types of second mortgages: home equity loans and home equity lines of credit. Home equity loans typically don't have pre-payment penalties, but you have to check the loan documents to be sure. Home equity lines of credit almost always have an early closure fee, typically between $250 and $500. Again, you have to check the specific wording and keep in mind that rules vary from state to state.

So what do you do if your client isn't sure? The best thing is to review their loan documents with them. Pre-payment penalties are usually spelled out on a separate document from the actual note and trust deed. If documents can't be located, then put the title company on alert that you need payoffs quickly so you can determine the client's accurate mortgage debt.

SALES COMMISSION

This is just the straightforward calculation of your sales commission. You've agreed to be paid when the home sells, usually a percentage of the final sales price. Many real estate offices are now assessing transaction fees. If yours is one of them, be sure to include that fee in your calculation.

TITLE INSURANCE FOR BUYER

It is standard and customary that a seller provide a buyer with a title insurance policy called an owner's policy. Rates vary from state to state on varying types of coverage and are based upon the sales price of the home. If your listing is selling for $250,000 your client could be looking at a title policy expense of approximately $1300. It's not a detail you want to leave until the last minute. Your local title company can provide you with a convenient, reduced-size rate chart that you can keep with you to better estimate this expense.

CLOSING AND RECORDING FEES

Whether you are closing with an escrow officer or an attorney, there will be some or all of following: closing fee, document preparation fee, attorney fee, notary fee, city, county or state tax fees or stamps, and recording fees. You'll have to familiarize yourself with standard fees in your area and how to calculate them.

UTILITY ASSESSMENTS

Title/escrow companies will check with local utility providers of water, sewer, sanitation, etc. to verify that these charges are current and paid up through to the closing date. Homeowners' association (HOA) dues will also be verified, when applicable, to make sure that all assessments are satisfied. If any of these are not current, they will be charged to your seller at closing. Hopefully, these amounts are small and not of major impact, but the question is important. A condo owner with a $170 monthly condo fee who is selling due to financial difficulty could take a substantial hit if fees haven't been paid in several months.

PROPERTY TAX PRO-RATION

This is another market-specific item. Quite often, property taxes are paid in arrears. For example, here in Utah we pay property taxes for the current year in November. That means that up until November every seller is going to have to pay a pro-rated amount of property taxes to the buyer to compensate them for the November tax bill that will be coming their way. The new owner will be liable for the entire bill when it is issued, even though they didn't live in the home the entire time. This is where the tax pro-ration comes in. They get the old owner's portion of the bill in credit at closing. Again, do your research. Find out how much the property taxes are and learn how to estimate these pro-rations.

BUYER'S CLOSING COSTS

Depending on your local real estate market and customs, a seller paying all or a portion of a buyer's closing costs may or may not be common. The majority of loan programs allow a seller to pay an amount equivalent to at least 2% (sometimes as high as 9%) of the sales price toward a buyer's closing costs and pre-paid items. If your seller has agreed to pay, it can easily mean a bottom-line impact of $3000 to $8000—not a small detail to overlook. If it is a common practice in your local market, this can also be a great opportunity to educate the client on the likelihood of this expense from the beginning. Full disclosure and reality check: just another reason they will love you.

HOME WARRANTY

Home warranties offer a buyer protection for the first year of home ownership against component failures of the home.

Furnace, water heater, stove, air conditioning units, etc. can be covered under this warranty. Coverage options vary from one warranty company to another but this added blanket of protection can be attractive to potential buyers. There are no set rules on who pays for this. I've seen buyers opt to purchase the coverage at their own expense. Sometimes sellers offer to pay for it as an incentive to the listing. My personal favorite is the Realtor who offers to provide the coverage as part of his or her superior service and commitment to the client. (What a great marketing tool for a Realtor to grab attention from prospective sellers and buyers!) Costs are usually $300 to $400. Talking to sellers early about home warranty coverage and preparing them if it's standard in your market for a seller to provide it will just be another feather in your cap.

JUDGMENTS/DEBT PAYOFF

This line item takes into account any outstanding judgments against the sellers that a title company and lender will require be cleared at settlement, and/or any debt that must be paid in order for this settlement to go forward or to help the seller qualify to purchase a new home. Sometimes there are equity payoffs to ex-spouses that were agreed to in previous divorces.

In Chapter 1, I talked about bankruptcy and how judgments dismissed against someone personally in a Chapter 7 filing may still stand as a lien against his or her property.

This is one reason why the "B" question can be so important when listing a home.

Another little known fact is that title companies and lenders usually require that all judgments associated with the sellers be cleared at settlement. This really took one buyer by surprise. Here's what happened:

A Realtor and fellow writer called me one day and said, "Tracey, I've got a story for your book." He went on to explain that a seller on a current listing was just informed by the title company that his disregard for child support payments had finally caught up with him. (They, of course, used more professional and delicate wording.) The seller was expecting about $35,000 in profit at his settlement. However, the $30,000 outstanding judgment from the state child support enforcement authority was going to reduce that profit considerably. The seller didn't mention this issue at listing and was apparently thinking it didn't matter. The Realtor had no way of knowing until the title company found the judgment, as they are not recorded against real property on the county records. Occasionally, a lien that is recorded against property will go on to court to become a judgment, but in most cases, judgments are for debts not associated with real property. So the seller went forward with the sale, but not in a cheery fashion.

OTHER

This is the catch-all line where you put any other concessions the seller has agreed to pay. This could include paying for the home inspection, termite inspection, a carpet and paint allowance, or maybe a repair escrow. Repair escrows are usually associated with FHA or VA loans that have specific property condition standards. If the necessary repair cannot be completed prior to closing, usually due to inclement weather, a repair escrow is established so funds are available to complete repairs as soon as possible.

Using this net sheet will walk you and your sellers through some important considerations as they list their home. Hopefully, the bottom line is appealing or at least acceptable to the sellers. The worst case scenario is that, after going through the numbers, your sellers realize that they cannot afford to sell at this time. Figuring this out from the start can be a huge time and money saver for you and your client. They'll remember you when their personal position improves. You'll be the agent they love.

CHAPTER 3

Pre-Approval Letters: Reading Between the Lines

Let's go back and revisit the Millers. You remember them, the cute couple who love you and everything you've done for them. Let's say that you have multiple offers for their house coming in on the same day. How do you help them analyze these offers beyond the obvious consideration of offer price? How can you guide them to a successful settlement with a quality buyer?

The first rule to remember is, talk is cheap. Many agents out there will write up an offer for *anybody*. They use the spaghetti-cooking approach to real estate (as do many loan officers): Throw it at the wall and hope it sticks. An offer does not guarantee that a buyer has been pre-approved by a lender. An offer doesn't guarantee that the buyer can get approved for a mortgage. It just says, "Hey, we like your house and would like to buy it for this price." That's nice, but it doesn't necessarily get the Millers to the settlement table.

Purchase contracts allow a loan application deadline, implying that a buyer can start the loan process after an offer has been accepted, but this probably isn't the best course of action for a buyer and it really puts the seller in a waiting game. That being said, I know lots of excellent Realtors who are very good at asking some key questions and moving forward with an offer for buyers who, for whatever reason, haven't started the loan process yet. They turn out to be great borrowers and all is well.

A competitive market dictates a much more aggressive preparation for any buyer hoping to get an accepted offer on a property. The buyer should visit his or her loan officer and get fully pre-approved. The loan officer should issue the buyer a letter of pre-approval or notify the Realtor of the pre-approved status so that a more "custom" letter can be provided upon making an offer on a home. This custom pre-approval letter would match the sales price of the offer and any of the contingencies of the transaction, e.g., sale and closing of the existing residence, seller to pay $3000 toward buyer's closing costs and prepaid items, etc.

Okay, back to you and the Millers. You need to review these offers with them and determine the best choice. You'll be considering sales price, sales contingencies, settlement dates, and buyer quality. Suppose you've got two similar offers, each with an accompanying letter of mortgage loan status. One says that Buyer A is pre-qualified. One says that Buyer B is pre-approved. Which one is better and how can you tell?

If every loan officer worked the way I wish they did, they should be able to glance at these two letters and say, "Ah ha! Buyer B has a pre-approval letter and must be the best." Pre-approved is better than pre-qualified, right? Let me give you some insight from the lending side of the fence that will open your eyes to the wishy-washy world of mortgage.

PRE-QUALIFICATION LETTERS

A pre-qualification letter implies many different degrees of thoroughness in regards to determining a buyer's borrowing ability. It may indicate that a credit report has been pulled and reviewed, but no other information has been verified. The loan officer simply used verbal information provided by the buyer, almost always over the phone. This is very common. Or the pre-qualification letter may be the result of a five-minute conversation with a loan officer that went something like this:

> *Loan Officer:* Mr. Buyer, can you tell me about your credit history?
> *Potential Buyer:* No problems that I know of.
> *Loan Officer:* Great. Are you employed?
> *Potential Buyer:* Yes.

Loan Officer: And how much do you make per hour?

Potential Buyer: I make $19.00 per hour.

Loan Officer: Wonderful. And how about regular monthly payments?

Potential Buyer: Well, I have a car payment of $125 per month and that's about it.

Loan Officer: Do you have any money you'd like to use as down payment?

Potential Buyer: No. I'm interested in 100% financing, like it says in your ad here in the phone book. Is this going to take long? I've got to meet my Realtor in 30 minutes to make an offer on a house and she said that you should email her my letter that I need to go with this offer. By the way, what's your interest rate?

Loan Officer: Well that depends on the loan program. Our state housing agency program is currently at 6.09%.

Potential Buyer: Okay, that sounds pretty good. My neighbor just bought a house and they said their rate was higher than that.

Loan Officer: What is the sales price on the home you are looking at?

Potential Buyer: $160,000.

Loan Officer: Okay then, that looks like it should be no problem. I'll send your letter over right now and let's make an appointment for you to come in the next few days.

That interview was full of so many holes from a practical standpoint that I don't even know where to begin. Then there's the issue of federal regulations that were violated. But let's stick to the stuff that affects you and the Millers. This conversation could very well be the basis of a pre-qualification letter you are looking at. It's not until much later when Mr. Buyer comes in for his loan appointment that the loan officer finds out that Mr. Buyer has two unpaid judgments and four collection accounts, none of which Mr. Buyer had knowledge of. He also discovers that Mr. Buyer does make $19.00 per hour at his job—the job he just started last week after being unemployed for the last eight months and at which he works only 20 hours per week. It also slipped Mr. Buyer's mind that he is obligated to pay alimony and child support in the amount of $650 per month (this was based off of his previous employment nine months ago).

Trust me that when you do the math on Mr. Buyer, he can't qualify for the $160,000 home your are trying to sell. So you have a pre-qualification letter that never should have been written in the first place and is now wasting both your and your client's time because of its lack of appropriate verification of the borrower's financial status.

Some letters of pre-qualification may be the result of a more comprehensive phone application process and represent a truly creditworthy buyer. It's usually very difficult to tell the good from the bad.

Now let's explore the pre-approval letter and all that it is supposed to represent.

PRE-APPROVAL LETTERS

It is generally accepted that a pre-approval letter should be a letter issued to a buyer based on a full review of the client's credit, income, and asset status. Hopefully, it also means that the applicant was processed through an automated underwriting system such as Fannie Mae's Desktop Underwriter. In that case, the loan officer would have taken a full mortgage application and have a well-documented file full of pay stubs, bank statements, proof of identity, signed disclosures, a good faith estimate, truth in lending documents, and a credit report. In short, the loan officer can offer a high level of certainty that the borrower is worthy and that the borrower is well informed of the financial requirements to close this loan and make the monthly payments.

Now let me introduce you to the root of all your problems in this area: the loan officer. I know that the loan officer is the problem child because I hear about other loan officers from Realtors all the time. I also know that it's the loan officer issuing the letters that you are trying to decipher right now with the Millers and there are no hard and fast rules regarding these letters that we (loan officers) have to follow. What should you do?

First, understand that a perfectly thorough loan officer may have issued the pre-qualification letter you have for Buyer A. This particular loan officer just prefers the term "pre-qualified" and doesn't get caught up in the terminology. She just focuses on doing a good job on her mortgage applications and serving her clients to the best of her ability. That's dandy.

Second, the pre-approval letter you have for Buyer B may not be worth the paper it's written on because, unlike our aforementioned loan officer lady, Buyer B's loan officer had a five-minute conversation not unlike the one previously presented, and likes to use the term pre-approved loosely. Very loosely.

Unless you have the good fortune of personally knowing the loan officers issuing both of the letters and have great confidence in either mortgage professional, your next step is to read each letter carefully for answers to these questions:

1. Does the letter state the actual sales price of the home the buyer is approved to purchase? (If they offered $200,000 but are only approved to $190,000, there's a problem.)

2. Does it state that the buyer's credit status, income, and assets have been verified? (Buyers doing stated-income and/or stated-asset loans wouldn't need income or asset verification, but you won't know this just from the letter.)

3. Does it indicate if the buyer has been approved through an automated underwriting system?

If you can answer "yes" to all of these questions, I'd say you have a letter written by a competent, detail-oriented loan officer. But more importantly, the buyer represented in that letter is probably a solid borrower. If these questions aren't answered, call the loan officer for more details. Due to privacy laws and confidentiality issues, a loan officer will not give you any specifics, but they could answer the above questions and help shed some light on the strength of the offer your clients are considering.

Letters of pre-approval are never ironclad guarantees. This can be nerve-wracking sometimes because you don't want to accept the wrong offer and let the strong borrower get away, only to go back to that strong borrower later and be told, "Sorry. We've found another home."

Hopefully this little tutorial doesn't have you running to sign up for bank teller training school as you've decided that you don't want to continue hacking your way through the jungle of real estate anymore. Just like Realtors, mortgage professionals come in varying degrees of expertise and competency and, typically, you don't get to choose the lenders who affect your paycheck each month. (I'm not making you feel any better, am I?) Let me just say, go forth, Realtor Extraordinaire. Go forth with this knowledge to guide your clients through this real estate reality and be the agent they love. You'll be fine.

CHAPTER 4

Dates, Deadlines, and Details

Logistics is the planning and implementation of the details of an operation. In the real estate world, this means who does what when. From response times at the beginning of the offer process to loan application, inspection, appraisal, and loan denial deadlines during the transaction, you have a lot to keep track of when a contract gets written, considered, and accepted. When it comes down to the wire, you've got settlement, funding, recording, and, most important, possession to worry about. The smoothest transaction in the world can end in anger and confusion when logistics are not considered. Sometimes a transaction never gets off the ground because of poor logistical planning.

The three primary reasons you, as the buyer's agent, may be the target of this anger and confusion are:

1. The buyer's offer has been rejected.
2. The buyer loses his or her earnest money.
3. The buyer is not able to move in when expected.

While contracts vary and special provisions can be written in for "nonrefundable" earnest money, some of the deadlines we'll be discussing provide an "out" for buyers. This out allows them to cancel the contract and leave the transaction with their earnest money in hand. Violate a deadline, however, and the seller may get to keep your earnest money.

Every state's purchase contract is different, so I won't even attempt to dissect a certain state's form. I will instead go through some common deadlines and take a look at how you can avoid problems as you go. When questions or discrepancies arise, always consult with your broker and/or legal counsel.

Also, keep in mind that this book is written from the perspective of a loan officer, so my major concerns are to provide you with a look from my side of the fence. This is based on my own experiences and those of people I've interviewed, usually with mortgage, title, and client service lessons in mind. While I think you'll find this information very helpful, there most likely will be a whole other set of details you have to consider on every contract that have to do with the internal processes of your own office: updating MLS listings, getting contracts to transaction coordinators, sending escrow instructions, etc. Make sure you understand this internal system as well to keep all parties in the loop and on course.

OFFER/COUNTEROFFER/ADDENDUM RESPONSE TIMES

I had an agent tell a client once that the response times on the contract were really more of a guideline, not a true hard-and-fast rule. Those of you out there who've experienced a hot, fast-moving market are shaking your heads right now. You can tell stories of listings you've had with multiple offers where it was *all* about response deadlines. Many of you have probably had a least one listing where the buyer to whom you made a counteroffer missed out because of an agent who didn't move quickly enough.

The other side of the coin is a sharp buyer's agent who is fully aware of the impending deadline, but has a buyer who either can't be reached or just doesn't get the urgency of the situation. Sometimes buyers can be reached by phone and want to accept the counter, but aren't available for signature within the deadline. That's where your reputation with your colleagues and knowledge of the standard practices in your area will determine the outcome. Verbal acceptances with promises of "signatures coming" can be tricky business.

LOAN APPLICATION DEADLINE

Hopefully, you are representing a buyer who is fully pre-approved and this is not a worry. The offer you are writing will always be stronger with a pre-approval letter attached. If pre-approval hasn't happened yet, be sure to discuss the importance of moving quickly. I've had many agents request the name of the client's preferred lender while they were writing the contract so that they could call and make the application appointment right then. If the preferred loan officer is out of town and won't be available for ten days, it's nice to know. A decision needs to be made on whether to try pushing out the deadline (not a great idea) or looking for an alternative lender.

INSPECTIONS DEADLINE

Coordinating home, termite, and septic inspections can be quite the juggling act. Throw in a water test, if necessary, and things become even more complicated. The property, local requirements, buyer's preferences, and lender requirements will dictate what the word "inspection" means. This is just another example of how knowing your area and coordinating with a lender early can be central to a smooth transaction. You've got to figure out what inspections your client wants or needs and how long they will take to complete.

Home Inspections

While a professional home inspection is always advisable, a client may choose not to have one, or may want to do their own inspection. If they want a professional report, hopefully you are familiar with the availability of inspectors in your area and a general turnaround time.

Termite Inspections

Do we need/want one or not? In some areas termite inspections are an unwritten rule on any property because termites are a common problem. If a professional home inspection is done, the termite inspection is usually already part of the service. Many times your loan type dictates what is required.

Utah is a great example of the term "it depends" when it comes to termite inspections in conjunction with loan requirements. While we have termites in Utah, they are not a common problem and termite inspections are not automatically requested by a buyer. Typically, if a buyer is doing a conventional loan on a property, a termite inspection is not needed. The exception may come when an appraiser notes in the appraisal that there were signs of infestation. (This would be a rare fluke because appraisers are not going into a home looking for termites; it's not their job. But if they see something obvious, they are supposed to note it in the appraisal. Then the reviewing underwriter will want the home inspected and treated if necessary.)

One other exception would be when an underwriter reviews an appraisal and notices in the pictures of the home that there is direct wood-to-ground contact. Many seasoned underwriters will ask for a termite inspection in this instance.

Veterans Affairs (VA) loans and Federal Housing Administration (FHA) loans have completely opposite requirements. This is a new twist for lenders in Utah because VA and FHA have always been very similar in their property standards. FHA recently dropped its termite inspection requirement for Utah. Last year we had to have them; this year we don't. Again, unless an appraiser notes a problem or an underwriter requires one, termite inspections are no longer part of the FHA loan process. VA loans, on the other hand, still require a termite inspection.

So, my advice on termite inspections is to know your area and/or call your buyer's lender to be sure.

Septic Inspections

For some of you who always deal with properties on public sewer systems, this will be a great bit of info for the property that's somewhere in your professional future and has a septic tank.

Some counties require septic inspections anytime a home is sold. These are usually conducted by a local municipal authority. They will be looking at: (1) flow (are the toilets flushing and the drains draining); (2) any signs of improper leach field function (standing water/sewage in the yard); and (3) whether the tank has been pumped in the last five years. If not, that will have to be done.

FHA loans require a septic inspection only if there are signs of system failure or if an underwriter or local authority requires it. VA wants a septic inspection if there are known soil percolation problems, or the local authority or underwriter requires it. Conventional loans are dependent upon the individual underwriter, but they are usually required.

If the septic tank needs to be pumped, a whole different set of considerations enters the picture. This is great dinner conversation and warrants taking some extra time for a few fun-filled facts. First of all, it is rare that a homeowner remembers or even knows that it is advisable to have a septic tank pumped every five years, especially if the septic system is older. Newer tanks are much more efficient but won't be exempt from pumping if it is a loan or municipality requirement. The party really starts when the homeowner realizes that in order to get the tank pumped, they have to locate the tank, and, more specifically, the opening to the tank. Nine out of ten owners don't even know where their tank is on their property. Sometimes you can go to the county and the system will be on record with a plot plan of the tank so you can locate it. Many times I've had sellers out digging up half their backyard trying to find the septic tank. This gets especially interesting in some regions in January when the ground is frozen.

Now for the really good news: Technology has left no corner of the professional world untouched. It has even found its way into the septic system business. I discovered this last year when I had a buyer for whom I was doing a loan, and who was also selling a property without the assistance of a Realtor. My client was notified by his buyer that their loan required a septic inspection and since they had lived there ten years and never pumped the tank, a tank pump as well. My client called me to (a) confirm that this was a normal lending requirement, and (b) lament loudly about the fact that they had no idea who to call for service, what it was going to cost them, or where the tank was located.

It just so happened that I was familiar with a septic service company in his area but couldn't remember what they charged. For whatever reason, my client felt too overwhelmed to make a phone call and asked me to please call them and find out the cost and call him back. Hey, customer service, right? So I make the call and during the conversation was informed that they offered a tank locating service as well. For a mere $60 they would drop a ball in the toilet that gives off a radio signal. They would then flush the toilet and follow the signal out to the backyard until it stopped. Tank located. But here's the best part. They offer a $20 rebate if you'll retrieve the ball and return it to them. Is that a deal or what!?

Water Tests

A water test could be required on a private water system (a well) for many reasons. Some jurisdictions require it. Your buyer may want it or it may be customary to the area.

An FHA loan requires it only under certain conditions, i.e., mining or heavy agriculture within a quarter of a mile, underwriter discretion, etc. VA will want it no matter what. Conventional loans may want it at the underwriter's discretion and most underwriters will want one. Lack of potable water means major problems with marketability and value.

APPRAISAL DEADLINE

Okay, so now you have all your inspections figured out and have come up with a reasonable deadline date. Now it's time to worry about the appraisal deadline. Time frames can really vary from area to area. Many areas are saturated with appraisers and turnaround times are within a week. Other areas, either because of lack of appraisers or an especially busy market, are dealing with a three-week minimum wait for an appraisal. In rural areas, long waits are especially common.

Wait times can also be lender specific. You would think that since the lender orders the appraisal, they would just use whatever appraiser is fastest. Most lenders will only work with certain appraisers that are on their approved list or ones with whom they have ongoing relationships. If those appraisers are swamped, everybody waits. Knowing general timetables for your area will help, but it's always better to check with the lender if you can. One other note is that with VA loans, the lender doesn't get to choose the appraiser. The VA automated appraisal system assigns the appraiser to the property. While VA has recommended turnaround times for their VA-approved appraisers, there are no guarantees.

LOAN DENIAL DEADLINE

To be practical, this date should be far enough after the appraisal deadline to allow for what we call final underwriting. A loan can't have a final approval without the appraisal, so the lender can't go forward with this step until the appraisal is available. How long for final underwriting? That, too, can depend from lender to lender. For some it's three days; for others it will be two weeks. If you haven't researched this with the buyer's specific lender, you may be creating a deadline that can't be met. This would, therefore, put your buyer at a higher risk for losing their earnest money if something goes wrong.

I can argue for two different approaches to loan denial

deadlines. From the seller's perspective, dragging out a loan denial date means that a buyer can tie up the property for a longer period of time, have their financing denied, and still get their earnest money back. While a seller's property isn't taken off of the market, the status of "under contract" tends to scare off any other interested parties. Not getting to keep the earnest money is sort of like adding insult to injury if everything falls apart at the end. While no amount of earnest money is going to make up for a lost sale, at least it's something. As a seller's agent you may want to lobby for as short a deadline as possible when reviewing an offer with your client.

Buyers, on the other hand, always have the possibility of last-minute loan denial due to completely unforeseen circumstances. I've had buyers scheduled for settlement on a Monday who got laid off from their jobs on the previous Friday afternoon. It doesn't seem fair to take their earnest money when they've just suffered such a financial blow. To protect them from losing their earnest money, a loan denial date as close to the settlement date as possible is the way to go. Then the question becomes, will the seller accept it?

SETTLEMENT DATE

This is the day when buyer and seller sign documents. Most of us call this "closing," but we are usually wrong. Closing isn't until the loan has actually been funded by the lender (and the title/escrow company has the funds) and then recorded at the county recorder's office. At that point, the transaction is actually closed.

Figuring out the best settlement date for your buyer means you have to work backward. You first have to ask the question, "Exactly when do you want to take possession?" You have to start with the day (and time of day) your client wants to take possession and work backward from there. This is absolutely critical for the buyer who is selling a home simultaneously and trying to orchestrate a smooth move from one house to the other. Get this one wrong and you can have a buyer sitting curbside in front of their new home in a U-haul they can't unload and is supposed to be returned to the rental place in four hours. Not to mention the fact they have nowhere to sleep that night.

First you consider any number of days or hours that the seller has requested to retain possession after closing. Example: In a counteroffer, the seller wants to relinquish possession 48 hours after recording. Now calculate the time it takes to record. Some escrow companies have the ability to record electronically, so recording can happen within minutes of receiving funds. Most escrow companies still have to physically take the documents to the recorder's office. Depending on how they schedule their personnel, this can mean the difference between a 4:58 p.m. recording on Thursday afternoon and a 10:00 a.m. recording on Friday morning. That means instead of moving into the home on Saturday evening at 5:00 p.m., they have to wait until 10:00 a.m. on Sunday morning, if the seller is not flexible.

Funding can really foul up a closing—thanks, again, to your local flaky lender. Every lender handles their funding differently. You have to hope that whoever is in charge of doing this funding has shown up to work today, and if she hasn't, you have to hope that someone is supposed to be a backup. I had a funding once that took three days to materialize. I was a loan officer in a brokerage so I was dependent upon the funding department of the lender to whom the loan was brokered. (This was many years ago, and I have since moved on to be with a mortgage banker that controls our fundings in-house.) The point here is you need to talk to the lender, get a time frame, and then pray that it happens.

Funding, recording, and possession practices vary from state to state. Some states expect "table fundings." In other words, the loan money beats the client to the settlement table. When loans are table funded, buyers can get the keys to their home that same day. In Utah, loans are typically funded and recorded the next business day after settlement. Buyers get their keys then or at the agreed-upon possession date after recording.

Take special care with out-of-state buyers. If they've bought and sold a home before they often assume that everything works the same in every state. This is how you and your clients can arrive at the "anger and confusion" point I mentioned at the beginning of this chapter. Again, when writing an offer, don't ask, "What day do you want to settle/close?" Instead ask, "What day do you want to take possession?" and work from there.

Once a contract is accepted, be sure that you or your staff log all of your contract deadlines and follow up on each one. A good loan officer will be doing the same. By calendaring these items at the beginning, you can relax and work through the transaction, confident that you are representing your buyer brilliantly!

CHAPTER 5

Bankruptcy: Clear Up Misconceptions

Don't people have to wait seven years after a bankruptcy to get a mortgage approval? Don't I have to finish my payments on my Chapter 13 before I apply for a home loan? I heard sub-prime lenders will give me a loan one day out of bankruptcy? What's the real story here? Well, like everything else in mortgage, we come back to the same answer: It depends.

I need to explain something about mortgages. A mortgage is almost always created under guidelines that will make it a saleable commodity. Who it is being sold to determines what the guidelines are. The information I'm sharing with you regarding bankruptcies is fairly standard practice that I see across the board, especially with FHA and VA loans. FHA, VA, and state housing loan guidelines are clear. When you start looking at sub-prime and conventional loans, you can really have some variance depending on the loan program and who the lender is eventually going to sell the loan to. Do you see why my answer to many questions is always, "It depends?"

In Chapter 1, I discussed how a bankruptcy can affect a seller. This chapter will give you some insight on how it affects borrowers. A little knowledge on this subject can really help with that common scenario Realtors so often find themselves in: Saturday afternoon buyers who haven't been pre-approved.

Whether you are sitting at an open house, or someone calls on your listing, it's very possible they will start throwing out life stories and loan questions. While you always want to instruct them to seek out a competent lender, some basic information may help you impress a potential new client. It may also save you from spending time with a client who's not quite ready for mortgage approval.

Again, a lender will have to make that final determination, but there's no sense staying up until midnight writing an offer for a buyer who's still in the middle of a Chapter 7 bankruptcy. Instead, take the opportunity to add these folks to your list of future prospects. An encouraging call every couple of months will let them know you are committed to helping them become homeowners. A good lender can guide them to a point where they will be ready for that big day.

How a bankruptcy affects a mortgage application depends on a number of things:

1. What type of bankruptcy is it? Chapter 7 or Chapter 13?
2. When was it filed?
3. Has it been discharged? When?
4. Was it filed exclusively for relief from medical bills?
5. What type of loan is being sought? Sub-prime, conventional, FHA, VA, or state housing?

Let's start by saying that we are going to look at the rules for buyers and not borrowers who are refinancing their home. The rules are pretty much the same for both, except with sub-prime loans. If a loan is super-low risk—i.e., low loan-to-value, borrower with stable income, etc.—sub-prime lenders can be more lenient on a refinance transaction. With the upheaval of the sub-prime market at the beginning of this year, they've tightened up a lot. When it comes to purchase loans, they've tightened up their requirements so much that their rules are almost the same as all other types of lending. So why put a buyer in a higher interest rate, sub-prime loan when they can qualify for a conventional, FHA, VA, or state housing loan?

Sub-prime, FHA, VA, or state housing loans will usually follow the same general guidelines for each type of bankruptcy.

• *Chapter 7*: The bankruptcy must be discharged (not filed) a minimum of two years ago. If the bankruptcy was filed exclusively for the relief of medical bills, then the time limit is a minimum of one year from discharge.

- *Chapter 13*: A borrower must have made at least 12 on-time payments to the Trustee. The bankruptcy does not have to be discharged.

A "conventional loan" is a blanket term that could cover a community homebuyer program that has less stringent credit requirements, as well as a niche loan such as stated income. The loan type and risk level will determine whether the bankruptcy rules are the same as above or more stringent. On a higher risk loan you could easily have a "no-bankrupt-cies-filed-or-discharged-within-the-last-four-years" rule. So once again, my standard answer—it depends—really applies.

I have worked with many clients over the years with bankruptcies in their credit history. Many who just barely cleared the "wait period" requirement, but still qualified for 100% financing under a VA, Community Home Buyer, or state housing loan. I've also denied many loans for borrowers with previous bankruptcies. Many denials were given to borrowers who were four years or more past their discharge date. What are the differences between the two groups of borrowers?

- *Re-established Credit.* Borrowers who have had a bankruptcy must prove themselves creditworthy again. Many times they did not include a car loan in the bankruptcy and have continued to make on-time payments. Sometimes they've opened a credit card account, even if they had to do it by securing the card with savings. These two methods are the most common ways borrowers keep good credit reporting to the credit bureaus, thereby raising their credit score over the two-year period since the bankruptcy. They also have taken care to pay all other obligations on time to avoid having any new collection accounts or judgments.

- *Reserves.* This is what lenders call money in the bank. We also consider retirement and investment accounts in the reserve tally. Let's say that a borrower is trying to qualify for a home and the total house payment is $1200. If they have $1200 in savings, we then view that as "one month's reserve"; $2400 would be two months, and so on. Reserves can always be the difference between an approved or denied status. Because lenders use automated underwriting software we can not only enter in a client's current application information, we can enter future information as well. I may get a "denied or refer" decision on an applicant who has no reserves. I can then re-enter the amount of money he hopes to save over the next 90 days. One month reserve may change that underwriting decision to "approved," and now my client knows his clear-cut path to his goal of an approved loan.

One more quick comment: Did you know that if a client has used a credit counseling service and it reflects on their credit report, that fact must be treated with the same rules as a Chapter 13 bankruptcy?

While Chapter 7 bankruptcy filing rules have drastically changed in recent years, which will probably result in fewer future bankruptcies, there is a current buyer pool with an all-time high rate of bankruptcy in their credit histories. Understanding how this will affect their future home purchasing abilities is vital to assisting them in obtaining their dream and having you to thank for it!

CHAPTER 6

Divorce and Separation

Divorce and home sales go hand-in-hand. As parties go their separate ways, old residences are sold and new ones are purchased. The financial reality of divorce can bring a real estate agent or loan officer into the situation even before other family members. As a loan officer, I've found myself at the other end of a whispered conversation where a client is trying to determine what kind of home-buying power he or she will have after the divorce, without the kids overhearing.

Now comes the question, "Why does marital status matter?" Well, in the world of mortgage lending, divorce and separation open a gigantic can of worms. Divorce typically creates, eliminates, or assigns debt and income for each party. A mortgage lender has to combine this legal document with a borrower's application, income and asset documentation (pay stubs, bank statements, etc.), and credit report to get the true financial picture. Separation indicates that a divorce may be coming, and some kind of legal document is necessary to determine what the new financial picture will be.

Now combine emotional and sometimes irrational clients with the reality of a specific set of guidelines regarding their loan applications. Top that off with the fun fact that they have no idea these guidelines exist, and we have a deal killer on the horizon. The good news is that several things can be done before, during, and after a divorce to keep your client's borrowing ability intact. All he or she needs is for you to slip on your tights and cape and save the day by passing on this information. (Keep in mind that my tips best fit middle-class folks, not Donald and Ivana.)

BEFORE THE FIRST MEETING WITH AN ATTORNEY/MEDIATOR

Tell your clients that getting a handle on assets and debts is vital to the process. Monetary assets, stocks, bonds, retirement accounts, etc. can usually be identified and listed by gathering the last statements or looking up balances online. Create a list of all real estate owned (including addresses), automobiles, other vehicles, and personal property.

Now they need to get a copy of their joint credit report

from all three bureaus, Equifax, TransUnion, and Experian. They can go to the FCC-approved website www.annual creditreport.com; consumers are entitled to one free report per year from this site. These will be separate reports from each bureau and they can be a little confusing because they may not match because creditors don't always report to all three bureaus. They also can get a combined report from a fee-based site such as www.creditreport.com. This combined report may be a whole lot easier to read and worth the money spent.

Next, list all debts, corresponding account numbers, and the asset secured by the debt. It's also helpful to note if an account is a joint account or not.

DURING THE DIVORCE PROCESS

1. *Advise clients to carefully review the way debt division is written in the decree.* They should especially be on the lookout for vague language such as "Petitioner is responsible for the following indebtedness: her Visa, her Citibank, and her Atlantic Bank accounts . . ." (Yes, I have witnessed language this vague.) This creates havoc when they have two Chase cards, three Citibank cards, and three loans with Atlantic Bank, all of them joint. The client may understand which accounts they were talking about, but an underwriter won't. Clarify!

Here's the deal: Mike made an offer on a home and it was accepted. He visited his lender. He completed a loan application, and his credit report was pulled and reviewed by the lender. He disclosed that he was divorced. He had provided all of the necessary documents for his loan file except a copy of his divorce decree. His lender issued a letter of pre-approval based on the preliminary information but asked him to bring in the divorce decree ASAP. Ten days later, Mike finally locates his divorce decree and takes it to his lender.

Here's the killer: Mike's credit report shows almost all of his debt as joint with his ex-wife. Mike has listed the debt that he knows he's responsible for on his application. However, because of very vague language it's impossible to understand which accounts are Mike's and which are his ex-wife's. To make things worse, Mike hasn't talked to his ex-wife in three years and they are not on speaking terms. Asking her to provide proof of payment for "her" debts to help clarify the debt structure is impossible. Because a lender can't determine the debt structure, Mike has to qualify with all of the debt.

2. *Explain the fact that they may be getting divorced, but their credit can still be married.* Joint debt activity is reported on both of their credit reports until the debt is paid off and the account closed, or refinanced into one name. This is bad news for the non-responsible party if there are late payments. The damage to their credit score could cost them a loan approval. Ugly, but true. If possible, advise eliminating all joint debt.

Suggest they monitor joint accounts by agreeing on access until they are paid off, closed, or refinanced. Internet access is convenient, but not always possible. They could inform creditors without websites of the situation and request both parties be notified in case of delinquency. Better they cough up the payment on an account that their ex can't pay this month than risk finding out later that their credit score is trashed.

Here's the deal: Jill's divorce decree clearly outlines which joint debts she must pay each month. She has always paid everything assigned to her on time. The joint debts assigned to her ex-husband have frequently been paid late. Jill assumes that the lender can clearly tell that she is creditworthy and will approve a loan.

Here's the killer: Jill's credit scores are extremely low. All joint debts are reported on her credit report and will continue to be reported until they are paid off. Due to the structure of the mortgage industry and the re-selling of mortgage loans to the secondary market, credit scores rule. Many secondary markets have credit score thresholds that must be met when reviewing a file for purchase. This stonewalls many lenders from approving a loan, even with "common sense" underwriting, because they have no market to sell the file to once it closes.

3. *Remind clients when listing children to include birth dates.* This will save them the hassle of providing birth certificates at loan application. Age determination is important. Guidelines allow child support income to be included only when it will continue for the next three years. In most

cases, this is until the child turns 18 or graduates from high school, whichever happens last.

Here's the deal: Mary calls a lender and explains that she gets $900 per month in child support and has been receiving that amount regularly for two years. She has monthly deposits into her checking account to support receipt. Her children are 9, 12, and 14. Her divorce decree doesn't state the children's birth dates, so she provides copies of birth certificates to prove the likely continuation of this income for the next three years.

Here's the killer: Mary waits 90 days before finding a home and her oldest child had a birthday 80 days ago. Now the 14-year-old is 15 and is scheduled to graduate from high school after turning 18. High school graduation is 33 months away. Mary no longer qualifies for the mortgage amount she wanted because the lender can only allow $600 (two-thirds) of the $900 income as stable and qualifying income.

4. *Are your clients trying to qualify and close on a home during the divorce?* Inform them that most lenders will require a legal separation agreement, especially if there are minor children involved. Lenders want something from the courts to get an accurate picture of potential debt division, alimony, and child support payments. If they are planning on using income awarded them in the agreement, they must provide a well-documented history of receiving the income for a period of three to twelve months, depending on

the lender's requirement. If they can't, they may be out of luck.

Here's the deal: Ellen is legally separated from her husband and has a court-signed separation agreement. She and her husband are selling their current home. She has good credit and a substantial down-payment for the new home she wants to purchase. She does not work outside the home and her only source of income is the $2600 alimony and child support payment she was awarded. The automated underwriting software has determined her to be a low risk and her loan approval only requires a three-month history of support payment documentation.

Here's the killer: Ellen privately agreed to allow her husband to live in the basement of the home they now occupy until the home is sold and they can both purchase separate residences. While staying there, he is paying all of the bills, but he is not paying her any alimony or child support. There is no track record of Ellen's sole source of income.

AFTER THE DIVORCE

Make sure your clients both have copies of tax returns for the last three years and copies of the signed divorce decree and any other important documents (e.g., bankruptcies, birth certificates, account statements, etc.). The need for these vital documents can slow down the loan application process when a spouse won't cooperate in obtaining copies.

Recipients of Child Support and Alimony

Again, stress to these clients that they should create a paper trail of alimony and child support income if they plan on using it to qualify. Payments made to them by cash or check should be deposited in their bank account. They shouldn't "hold back" money from the deposit or pocket the cash. They should deposit the entire amount and then withdraw funds afterward. Records from their local child support enforcement authority can be used as well to document income.

> *Here's the deal:* Debbie's ex-husband pays her $500 in child support each month in cash.

> *Here's the killer:* Debbie only deposits $100 each month and uses the remaining cash to purchase groceries and gasoline each month. Her bank statements only show a recurring deposit of $100. Her loan approval requires a six-month history of receiving the income. The lender can only "count" $100 as steady monthly income instead of $500. Debbie cannot qualify for the larger mortgage needed to purchase the home she wants.

Payers of Alimony

Make them aware that a verbal agreement to decrease payments will not help them decrease debt on a loan application. If changes are not documented through the court or the child support enforcement authority, the original payments declared in the decree will apply.

Here's the deal: John's divorce decree requires he pay his ex-wife $600 in alimony per month until her death or her re-marriage. John says that he is no longer required to pay the alimony because his wife is engaged and will be getting re-married in six months. She also has written a letter stating that she is waiving the alimony early.

Here's the killer: The letter from John's ex-wife cannot be used to dismiss the monthly debt. John has to qualify with the additional $600 in monthly debt until he can supply a copy of his ex-wife's marriage license or a court document that changes the current alimony award.

Payers of Child Support

Those clients who pay child support should also know that non-payment can drastically affect their credit report and their property title. (We talked about this in Chapter 1.) As state child support enforcement authorities use tougher legislation to collect support, non-payers have had rude awakenings when they've tried to sell their homes. Judgments filed by these authorities will show up on credit reports and/or be discovered during the title search process prior to closing.

Here's the deal: James is selling his condo. This condo was purchased after his divorce and he is the sole owner. James has not paid child support to his ex-wife in three years. A few days before closing, his agent calls to inform him that the title company has discovered a $36,000 back child support judgment filed against him. James claimed no knowledge of the judgment and it did not come up on his credit report.

Here's the killer: The title company will not close this transaction and issue the required title insurance without clearing this judgment. James must pay the judgment immediately and provide proof of payment, or the title company will hold the funds from his sale proceeds to satisfy the amount. James does not have the money to pay the amount and his total expected proceeds from the sale of this condo are only $10,000. As a result, he cannot sell this property.

Like them or not, those are the rules and realities of mortgage lending that can kill or delay a deal when divorce or separation is involved. Is there a way around some of the rules? Sure—by doing a different type of loan that doesn't require proof of income. Going this route just gets you around some of the income problems, but not all of the others mentioned. Borrowers will face more stringent credit and down payment requirements along with higher interest rates if they use these alternative loans.

Now here's some good news for you to share with a divorced single parent: Many state housing agency first-time homebuyer programs offer their low-interest 100% financing to single parents, even if they've owned a home in the last three years. This is a big deal. If you are not aware of your state's available program, it's time to get on board. These programs can be the answer for your single parents with no down payments, no money for closing costs, and low-to-average credit scores. For contact information for your state housing agency, refer to Appendix A.

The key to retaining your Realtor Extraordinaire status when the word divorce or separation gets mentioned is to get that client to a competent lender *now*. There is so much to sort out. Hopefully, sharing some of the above information will help them understand the impact of marital status and sources of income as they go forward to purchase new homes.

CHAPTER 7

Mortgage Approval Income Rules: Timing Is Everything

Because you are the agent they love, Ramon and Sara once again have called you to list their home. When you arrive, you can tell by their ear-to-ear grins that there is more going on than just selling a property. They are absolutely gushing about another home that they've seen in *the* neighborhood they've always dreamed about living in. They've already taken the virtual tour online and want you to make the appointment to take them to see it tomorrow. They just know it's the home for them—especially now.

"Now? Why? What's going on?" you ask.

"Well, it has the perfect guest house in back . . . to run our new business out of!" they practically shout. They are watching your face for the dawning of euphoria they know will overcome you at any moment as you grasp the meaning of their announcement.

"So you'll be leaving your jobs? Both at the same time, from your law firms?"

"Yes, we've both decided to give notice right away. Isn't it great? We're going to work from home together just like we always wanted."

"Aren't you worried about income?"

"We've been planning for this for quite awhile. We have some money saved up and we could always borrow against our retirement plans if we had to. We are going to use the profit from the house as our start-up capital. We'll just get 100% financing on the new house to conserve our cash. We've got great credit. We'll just do one of those stated-income loans. Our business plan is really solid and we should be profitable within the first year. We just can't wait to get started! Clothing design is our true passion!"

Prepare yourself for the roles you are about to take on— bubble-burster, killjoy, as well as wet blanket. However, what should boost your spirits about this moment is that you are getting involved now, instead of six months from now. Involvement now means that you can bring them up to speed on a few flaws in their plan. You'll still sell their house and help them buy their new house; they'll be happy and you'll get paid. That's pretty much their whole plan, isn't it? Six months from now they'd find out that the new house isn't a reality. Then you would not only be a wet blanket, but a wet blanket who gets paid nothing.

I will skip the obvious concerns of this situation—concerns such as both Sara and Ramon quitting their day jobs right away and how that may not be the best financial move; how maybe just one of them should quit; etc. I'm not their financial advisor and neither are you. In fact, there are many success stories that start with taking "the big risk." I wish them well. I look forward to seeing their labels on evening gowns I can't ever afford to buy (and have no place to go in them anyway).

As a voice of reason, you need to impress upon Ramon and Sara at this point that mortgage loans evaluate a borrower based on the following factors:

- Credit
- Amount and stability of income
- Debt-to-income ratios
- Reserves
- Loan-to-value (100%–103% being the highest risk)
- Property type and use (primary single-family residence being the lowest risk)

SPECIAL RULES FOR SELF-EMPLOYED BORROWERS

The problem with Ramon and Sara is going to be income stability and 100% financing. There are very different lending rules for self-employed borrowers, which they will be if they quit their jobs right now and start this business. Any loan program will allow self-employed borrowers, but there are certain hoops that they must jump through. There are special programs that are geared strictly for self-employed borrowers who have difficulty proving income, but they too have their hoops. These special programs are part of a group we call niche lending and they always have higher interest rates associated with them.

First, let's look at the standard income requirements for self-employed borrowers on conventional, FHA, VA, or state housing loans. These are the best sources of low- or no-down financing at the best interest rates possible.

- Borrowers must have been operating this business for at least two years in order to even consider income as stable and continuing, in other words, to even count it at all.

- Average monthly income is determined by analysis of federal tax returns and sometimes a current profit-and-loss statement.

Can you see the writing on the wall here for Ramon and Sara? Under the guidelines for these loans, if they quit their current employment, they will have no income for qualifying.

Many borrowers who satisfy the first requirement discover a major stumbling block with the second requirement. The problem lies in how underwriting guidelines require that a tax return or income statement be analyzed by the lender. When I'm taking an application and we start talking about business income, I've seen many a cheerful face suddenly sour when I use the phrase "net income."

I mention this phrase just after they've told me that they had $200,000 in income last year, because in their mind, this was their income. They assume that I'm going to look at their gross receipts from their latest tax return and use that number, which happens to be $200,000. This is a natural assumption, but it is wrong.

I have to go on to explain that underwriting guidelines require me to look at their net income, after expenses. A few expense items can be added back to the net income number, such as depreciation, but for the most part, net income is the number we are working from. Since most self-employed borrowers try to write off as much of their income as possible to decrease their income tax liability, we commonly see self-employed borrowers with $200,000 in gross receipts and $50,000 in net income. That's a big difference in buying power!

Niche Loans

Because this is so typical among business owners, the mortgage industry responded with niche loans that require no proof of income. These programs vary from stated income (borrower states their income, but no proof required) to no income or no doc loans, which require no income information at all, stated or otherwise. A borrower is judged strictly by their credit and assets, or sometimes just by their credit.

There are many versions of these types of loans, but three things hold true with this type of lending:

1. Interest rates are always higher.

2. Getting 100% financing under these programs has become impossible due to instability in the mortgage markets from increased foreclosures.

3. Many niche loans still want proof (business licenses or letter from CPA) that you have been in business for at least two years.

Loans are priced according to risk. These types of loans obviously carry higher risk so the interest rates go up. Since the beginning of 2007, the secondary market that buys loans has put the brakes on these higher risk products. They are experiencing high losses due to default and foreclosure and don't want the risk any longer. While stated income and no doc loans are still available, the loan-to-value and credit requirements have been tightened considerably.

Self-employed borrowers are not the only target for special guidelines. Income and timing rules apply to other types of job situations.

COMMISSION INCOME

Meet Melissa Wright. She just graduated from college. She has come to you to help her find the perfect condo. She's so excited to have a place of her own! Good thing she has great credit and is making lots of money each month at her new job—over $5,000 a month. She hasn't had time to save any money for a down payment, but that shouldn't be a problem with 100% financing. She seems like the perfect first-time homebuyer. She calls you on Friday afternoon. She can't get in to see a lender until Monday for pre-approval. You find the perfect condo on Saturday and write up the offer. All is well.

Not exactly. This is a scenario where I'm not going to have any deal-saving advice, only time-saving. The problem with Melissa isn't how much money she makes, it's how she makes it. She is a sales representative for a company that manufactures and distributes plumbing hardware. She is paid a base salary plus commission. Her base salary is $2,000 per month. Her commission makes up the other $3,000 per month. And the final blow is that she's only been employed for three months.

The guideline for commission income works like this: In order to count the commission part of the income for qualifying, the borrower must have a two-year history of earning commission. Many Realtors are already familiar with this rule because they face the same dilemma themselves when they decide to go into real estate, but want to qualify for a mortgage loan.

As Melissa's loan officer, I can only count her base salary of $2,000 per month as stable income. Niche lending isn't an option because of her limited time on the job and her need for 100% financing. Bottom line: She doesn't qualify for this condo.

RECENT GRADS ARE OKAY

Some of you may have thought that the fact that Melissa just graduated college was going to be a problem as well. There is good news on this subject you will want to pass along to potential buyers.

If a borrower has been attending school or training and then starts a new job after graduation, we do not have a "time-on-the-job" requirement. I have done loans for borrowers who just graduated from college and have only an official letter of hire. They didn't work during college. They haven't even started their new job, yet they closed on a home before they even got their first paycheck.

This is handy information to have when a young couple walks into your open house to "just look" because they're sure they can't qualify for a home loan. Not only may they qualify, but they may qualify for 100% financing with no out-of-pocket expense. Pretty cool, huh? Get them to a lender. Your just-looker recent grads may become buyers before the end of the month.

PROBATION PERIODS HURT

Since we are on the subject of new jobs, there is a potential deal killer when a client has started a new job—and it's not how long they've been on the job.

Thirty years ago, lenders wanted you to be at the *same* job for at least two years before they'd even consider you for a loan. Then you'd better have some hefty down payment to go along with that job. Today, as long as a borrower has been consistently employed (not necessarily with the same company) or attending school for the last two years, job change is not a bad thing. The bad thing is when that new job has a probationary period.

We usually uncover this when we have a borrower who hasn't started the new job yet or just recently started and doesn't have his first paycheck. We then ask to see their letter of hire to determine the amount and stability of income. If the letter indicates a probationary period, we cannot consider the income stable until after the probation period ends. This means we won't be able to close on a loan until after the probationary period has passed. Most probationary periods are for 90–180 days.

PREVIOUS EARNING HISTORY

The last situation we'll look at involves Josh and Amy, a couple you helped get into a little starter home a few years ago. They've outgrown this home and really need something a little larger.

They've been a little discouraged because home prices have been steadily increasing since they bought their first home and interest rates have gone up as well. They feel like they need to make a move now or a larger home may be out of their financial reach soon.

Josh is still at the same job and has had several small pay increases. Amy just went to work part time. They've looked at their budget and feel ready to take on a larger house payment, so they've called you, the agent they love, to list their home. (Okay, bubble burster, get ready to go to work.)

This is another case where you can only offer time-saving rather than deal-saving advice. While you always want to have a lender make the final determination, Josh and Amy may have a problem here.

Amy has always been a stay-at-home mom. She doesn't have any previous work history and has been working part time for six months. A lender typically can't count Amy's income for qualifying until she has a two-year history of working part time.

I've seen stay-at-home moms who dropped out of the workforce for five years to raise children. In some of those cases, because the person had previous higher-skilled employment (registered nurse, school teacher, etc.), we can accept her re-entry into the workforce and consider it stable. The issue lending guidelines have with new income is always the same: Is it stable and likely to continue? They want to see a track record that proves that a borrower can hold steady employment.

SECONDARY INVESTOR RULES

Before I end this chapter, I want to share another little known fact about mortgage lending. All loan programs have written guidelines, as you already know. The guidelines are created by FHA, VA, state housing agencies, Fannie Mae (Federal National Mortgage Association), and Freddie Mac (Federal Home Loan Mortgage Corporation). What most people don't realize is that every investor (companies who purchase and service mortgage loans), such as Countrywide, Suntrust, CitiMortgage, etc., may have their own set of rules for a program that are in addition to or in place of the existing rules.

Here's an example: FHA does not declare any minimum credit-score requirement for a borrower. They have specific credit guidelines, but do not declare a minimum credit score in these rules. Many investors are happy to purchase FHA loans, but they choose not to purchase loans with a credit score below 580. Many also charge higher interest rates for borrowers with scores below 585.

Loan officers are always trying to walk this tightrope between the primary rules and the secondary set of rules that the investors they are selling want to impose. While all of the information I've given you is true and correct for most lenders, you may find exceptions to any of the things I've mentioned.

NOT ALL UNDERWRITERS ARE THE SAME

One more cog in the lending machine is the underwriter. This is the individual who actually does the final loan approval. Underwriters are like you and me in that they are molded by their own professional experiences over the years. Their job is to evaluate the loan file and make sure that it follows the guidelines.

The guidelines, however, give the underwriter discretionary and interpretive powers. This is why, for example, one loan officer will ask a borrower for a divorce decree on a file and another one won't.

I had a particular situation where a borrower was separated but had no final divorce decree. My underwriter would not allow the loan to close without a copy of the divorce decree. The borrower went to another loan officer whose underwriter didn't require the divorce decree. The underwriter cited the fact that the borrower indicated that there were no children involved, so he felt comfortable letting a loan go forward without it.

My underwriter was more prudent in wanting the full financial picture before final approval would be given. That's her prerogative. I also happen to know that her decision was based on a reprimand she received during a file audit many years ago when she didn't get a divorce decree before approving a loan. She's covering her bases, protecting her job, and protecting the future owner of that loan. The investor who's buying that loan is counting on her to do just that.

Hopefully, this sheds some light on why there can be different answers to the same mortgage question. Why some borrowers can get approved and some can't. Why one loan officer wants a verification of rental history and one doesn't. Different programs. Different investors. Different underwriters.

My goal is to give you some basic heads-up warnings about potential problems that can happen with mortgage approval income rules, especially when employment changes and new homes happen at the same time. Frequently, you are the first call the client makes. They are unaware of the mortgage-qualifying consequences job changes can have. But once again, you can be the proactive thinker who gets them on the right path to the proper advisors so they can figure this out and purchase that dream home.

CHAPTER 8

Understanding FHA Loans Helps You Help Clients

FHA (Federal Housing Administration) financing is a great option for some buyers and a good marketing tool for your listings. Understanding this program can help you build your business and better serve all of your customers. Knowledge of FHA will also shed a lot of light on your state housing loans as well, since FHA is a commonly used loan within each state's first-time homebuyer programs.

FHA was created in 1934 to help stimulate the housing industry, which at that time was in dire straits. FHA doesn't actually provide loans to homebuyers; it provides mortgage insurance for loans that are made under FHA guidelines. In the last 60 years, FHA has insured over 34 million home mortgages and helped to bring the nation's homeownership rate to an all time high.

FHA has been so popular in the single-family housing market because of its low down-payment requirements (3% or slightly less), more relaxed credit standards, and higher debt ratio tolerances. While FHA loans have been a major part of the home financing picture for the last 60 years, they have seen a decline in market share over the last 10 years. There are several reasons for the downturn:

1. Development and expansion of A- and sub-prime lending

2. Higher profit margin of A- and sub-prime programs for lenders

3. Competing 100% financing options

4. No "property condition" requirements on other types of loans

5. No "allowable closing cost" restrictions on other types of loans

6. No "mortgage limit" restriction on other types of loans

A- and sub-prime lending programs help some homebuyers who couldn't have purchased a home any other way. Unfortunately, a large portion of the A- and sub-prime clientele was taken from the potential FHA pool of business. Why? For starters, FHA is a government agency and there are all kinds of rules and regulations that must be met in order for a lender to obtain FHA approval. It was easier to sell A- and sub-prime loan programs, avoid jumping through all the hoops, and make a lot more money.

Unfortunately, many of the borrowers who were put into these loans ended up with higher house payments, higher interest rates, variable interest rates, and pre-payment penalties. An FHA loan could have provided them with a lower monthly payment, lower fixed interest rate, and no pre-payment penalty. Are you starting to see some advantages here?

Then there's the lure of 100% financing. It didn't matter that this concept came along when interest rates were at historical lows. Even with slightly higher interest rates and higher mortgage insurance premiums, borrowers would rather pay $100 per month more for their home than shell out thousands up front on a down payment. Ask a seller to pay closing costs for you and *voila*, buyers slipped in with very little or no money at all.

The FHA Reform Act was approved by the U.S. House Financial Services Committee in May 2007. This legislation eliminates the 3% cash down requirement, making FHA a 100% financing product. The bill still has to be voted on by the House and the Senate, and I'm keeping my fingers crossed.

SOME DRAWBACKS TO FHA LOANS

Property condition requirements on FHA loans are probably the most well-known hurdle that directly affects your listings, and at times complicates your transactions. If a borrower is going to purchase your listing with an FHA loan, the lender orders an appraisal through an FHA-approved appraiser.

The FHA appraiser is trained not only to appraise the home, but also to go through a checklist of items pertaining to the home's condition. Any condition violations are noted on the appraisal. An underwriter will require that the conditions be remedied, preferably prior to closing. (Note: An FHA inspection is not as in-depth as a professional home inspection and should *never* be represented to a buyer as an adequate substitute for a home inspection.)

If a condition cannot be remedied prior to closing, an underwriter may allow a repair escrow to be set up to cover the cost of repair as soon as possible after closing. Long-term repair escrows are not allowed, so most underwriters allow 90 days for completion unless bad weather requires a longer wait time.

Repair escrow amounts are determined by taking the cost of the repair, per bid or appraiser estimate, and calculating 1.5 times the amount. The repair-escrow amount is usually deducted from the seller's funds at closing, held by the lender, and released upon a satisfactory completion report from the appraiser who did the original appraisal. The amount cannot exceed $5,000, which, under the 1.5 times calculation, would mean that your actual costs should be somewhere around $3,300.

FHA also used to have an "allowable closing cost" restriction that further limited its appeal to lenders and sellers. Lenders had two choices: Either don't charge a particular type of closing fee, which dropped their profit margin, or the preferred method of charging the fee to the seller and then hoping that the seller or their Realtor didn't squawk at closing. In 2006, FHA changed their policy to accept customary conventional fees and reasonable costs deemed necessary to close a mortgage.

FHA's widely used 2–1 buydown program also caused grief for sellers who were commonly asked to pay for the buydown so that the buyer could have a lower payment for the first two years of the mortgage. This 2–1 buydown meant that the interest rate was 2% lower than the note rate the first year, and 1% lower the second year. The third year of ownership, the payment adjusted to the note rate. Borrowers were allowed to qualify at the "bought down" interest rate of the first year, hence its huge popularity.

FHA also has mortgage limits. These limits vary by county. This restriction further reduces the number of properties available for FHA financing.

FHA LOANS ARE BETTER THAN EVER

Now let's get on to the nitty-gritty stuff on why FHA loans are a friendlier option for your listings.

FHA's response to lost market share was to relax its property standards in December 2005. In other words, they've gotten less picky when it comes to property condition.

They also changed their policy on allowable closing costs, basically opening the door for any charge that was "customary." Now lenders could stop pushing non-allow-able costs over to sellers and make more money on each loan.

FHA also re-wrote their qualifying requirements on their 2–1 buydown program in response to foreclosure trends they were seeing. The change still allowed 2–1 buydowns but required the borrower to qualify at the note rate, not the 2% lower start rate. That little adjustment slowed the activity on that program from a flood to a trickle. Why bother paying for a buydown if the borrower doesn't get the advantage of easier qualifying or qualifying for more home? So now it's rare that your seller will be asked to pay for a buydown.

The FHA reform legislation I mentioned earlier also has a provision to increase the mortgage limits to open up more homes to FHA financing. This will be another positive change for your listing marketability. For current mortgage limits, go to www.hud.gov. On the right hand side, click on Real Estate Brokers, and then on the left hand side, click on FHA Maximum Mortgage Limits. You can enter your state and county to get current information.

The big impact change here for you is the property standards issue. I can argue both sides of the fence on this change:

1. "But what about protecting the borrower? Relaxing standards just compromises the safety and security of the home."

2. "It's a garage window, for goodness sake. Why does my seller have to go through the hassle of having a cracked window on the back of the garage fixed? My

client wants to sell the house 'as is,' not have to deal with all of these silly minor repairs."

See? Both sides have their merits, but the reality is FHA was getting a bad rap and sellers facing multiple offers were steering away from FHA buyers.

Property Standards

Per FHA's Mortgagee Letter 2005-ML-48 the following property conditions *no longer require automatic repair for existing properties:*

- Missing handrails. Raise your hand if you've had a seller building the ugliest wood handrail to attach to the front porch of a house knowing full well that the buyer was just going to tear it down after it passed the FHA inspection. We certainly won't miss that one.

- Cracked or damaged exit doors that are otherwise operable

- Cracked window glass. Remember the back window of the garage in the example above? No worries now.

- Defective (chipped and/or peeling) paint surfaces in homes constructed after 1978. With no lead-based paint threat, the need to scrape and paint goes away. It's still not a good idea to let the kids eat paint chips, though!

- Evidence of previous (non-active) wood-destroying insect/organism damage where there is no evidence of unrepaired structural damage. If the termites have moved on and didn't eat too much while they were there, you're good to go.

- Rotten or worn out countertops

- Damaged plaster, sheetrock, or other wall and ceiling materials in homes constructed post-1978

- Poor workmanship

- Trip hazards (e.g., cracked or partially heaving sidewalks, poorly installed carpeting)

- Crawl space with debris and trash

- Lack of an all-weather driveway surface. This is good news for sellers in rural areas.

This next set of items are examples of conditions that *will continue to require automatic repair:*

- Inadequate access/egress from bedrooms to exterior of home

- Leaking or worn out roofs. If there are three or more layers of shingles on leaking or worn out roof, all existing shingles must be removed before re-roofing.

- Evidence of structural problems (such as foundation damage caused by excessive settlement)

- Defective paint surfaces in homes constructed pre-1978.

- Defective exterior paint surfaces in home constructed post-1978 where the finish is otherwise unprotected

Then the FHA Mortgagee Letter goes on to list items that *no longer mandate automatic inspections:*

- Wood-destroying insects/organisms: Inspection required only if there is evidence of active infestation, mandated by the state or local jurisdiction, or if inspection is customary to area, or at lender's discretion.

- Well (individual water system): Test or inspection is required if mandated by state or local jurisdiction; if there is knowledge that well water may be contaminated; when the water supply relies upon a water purification system due to presence of contaminants; or when there is evidence of:
  - Corrosion of pipes (plumbing)
  - Areas of intensive agriculture within ¼ mile
  - Coal mining or gas drilling operations within ¼ mile
  - Dump, junkyard, landfill, factory, gas station, or dry cleaning operation within ¼ mile
  - Unusually objectionable taste, smell, or appearance of well water (superseding the guidance in Mortgagee Letter 95-34 that requires well water testing in the absence of local or state regulations)

- Septic: Test or inspection is required only if there is

evidence of system failure, if mandated by state or local jurisdiction, if inspection is customary to area, or at lender's discretion.

- Flat and/or unobservable roof.

The last section of the Letter provides examples of conditions that will *continue to require automatic inspections.* (Note that required inspections must be performed by FHA inspectors, professional contractors, local authorities, or engineers depending on the item in question.)

- Standing water against the foundation and/or excessively damp basements

- Hazardous materials on the site or within the improvements

- Faulty or defective mechanical systems (electrical, plumbing, or heating)

- Evidence of possible structural failure (e.g., settlement or bulging foundation wall)

GUIDING YOUR SELLERS

Use the above information as a checklist on your next listing that falls within the FHA loan limits for your area. You can guide your sellers on pre-listing repairs and inspections and advertise that home with an FHA financing option. Even if a seller chooses not to make the repairs or have the inspections before they list the home, they'll be prepared for what's to come if they do get an offer from an FHA borrower. You will be helping them to open up their home to that additional group of buyers that FHA can provide.

You'll find your grasp on these changes especially helpful when you take a listing on a home where the seller's last home was sold to an FHA buyer 20 years ago. "We never want to go through that again! It cost us so much in points and extra fees and what a pain to do all those little repairs. Don't bring us any FHA offers!" Never fear! Now that you are armed with the facts about FHA, you will be able to expertly direct their focus to the "kinder, gentler" FHA of today.

A FEW CAVEATS

Having said all of that I do have a couple of quirks to share with you. The first has to do with property flipping. Again, due to fraud and in the interest of loss control, FHA analyzed those files and came up with the following rules (Mortgagee Letter 2006-14):

- Properties owned for less than 90 days are not eligible for FHA financing.

- Properties owned between 90–180 days will be subject to a mandatory second appraisal if the new sales price exceeds the previous sales price by 100%.

- Properties owned less than one year will be subject to additional underwriting scrutiny and possibly a second appraisal if the new sales price exceeds the previous sales price by 5%.

So, when taking a listing, keep these rules in mind as you determine the applicable financing options to list on the MLS. There are a couple of exceptions to this rule, so check with a knowledgeable FHA lender for the exact verbiage of the restriction.

This last piece of information is good to know at those inevitable Saturday open houses with those lookers who have all the finance questions. FHA (and VA) use a database that tracks individual borrowers when they incur a loss on a mortgage loan. This system is called CAIVRS (Credit Alert Interactive Voice Response System). Lenders must check the system on all borrowers of any FHA or VA loan. If someone had an FHA or VA loan that incurred a loss within the last three years, they are not eligible to do another FHA or VA loan until the three years have passed.

I had a client, Helen, who was trying to purchase a condo. She disclosed to me that she had co-signed on an FHA loan with her granddaughter several years earlier and her granddaughter got behind on the payments. The home was eventually sold, but she didn't know if there was actually a loss paid by FHA or not. Her credit report revealed a paid mortgage that had the notation "Foreclosure Redeemed." I assumed that the property was pulled out of foreclosure and then sold and was basically hoping that the notation was correct. Helen's credit and down payment situation made an FHA loan the best fit for her. Conventional financing was not an option and I wanted to avoid sub-prime financing.

My plan was derailed when the CAIVRS report revealed that there had been a loss paid on the home two years before. The lesson here is that co-signers are just as affected by these losses as the primary borrowers.

Even with all its hoops and rules, FHA is still a great loan program for many borrowers. If the new legislation passes, it will be easier than ever and open up doors for even more homebuyers. And those homebuyers (and sellers) will be well served having a Realtor like you who has FHA know-how!

CHAPTER 9

First-Time Homebuyer Programs: Beginner's Luck

First-time homebuyers are a gold mine: It's as simple as that. They are current clients, almost-guaranteed future clients, and the most enthusiastic source of referrals you could ever hope for. If you take care of them, chances are they will take care of you for years to come.

The most common first-time homebuyer programs are your state housing loans. Here in Utah, we have Utah Housing Finance Agency, Florida has the Florida Housing Finance Corporation, and so on. (Appendix A lists all of the state housing offices and their websites.) These agencies acquire their funds from the sale of tax-free bonds. If you are not plugged in to this resource, now is the time to learn.

State housing programs offer below-market interest rate loans to specific buyers (usually first-timers) who fall within the federal HUD (Office of Housing and Urban Development) median income level limits. Income level limits are established on a county-by-county basis. There are also sales price limits based on HUD median home price calculations for each county as well. Many states offer down payment and closing cost assistance that can mean 100% or even 103% financing for a borrower.

You can add to your loyal client base if you are willing to take a little time to learn some guidelines and be an advocate for these programs. Many Realtors like to offer first-time homebuyer seminars. Unfortunately, they tend to focus on everything except financing when the question uppermost in the homebuyer's mind is, "How can I get a loan and what will my monthly payment be?" Try partnering up with your state housing office to offer education that focuses on their loan program. Gather information on city/county/state down payment assistance grants. Bring in a lender who is an expert on state housing loans. You will fill some seats and reach some great prospects.

Here in Utah, we are lucky to have one of the most advanced, trendsetting state housing programs in the country. The strides this agency has made in the last six years are nothing short of amazing. They've taken a complicated, laborious process and turned it into a streamlined machine. My Utah Housing borrowers enjoy the same fast loan processing that I offer on any other loan program. While not all state housing agencies are the same or at the same point in their evolutionary progress, they still provide a great service to homebuyers.

I come across many Realtors who are less than enthusiastic about their state housing program, and there are some good reasons. They have war stories from years ago where buyers using state housing money delayed closings for various reasons. I can sympathize. Just know that these programs are worth a second look. Huge changes have taken place in many states. Enroll in your state's email notification list to keep you current on interest rates and program changes.

With 50 different state housing offices, each with independent programs, I can't provide you with specific details for your state. You will have to research that yourself. What I can do is give you some general information and some useful tips that might help save a deal, move a listing, or turn lookers into buyers.

WHO CAN USE A STATE HOUSING PROGRAM?

State housing programs are for first-time homebuyers—sort of. The definition is typically, "The buyer cannot have owned a home within the previous three years." But did you know that owning a mobile home that is not permanently attached to land and classified as real estate isn't considered home ownership? Did you also know that ownership of a rental property that you can prove you haven't lived in for the last three years may not be considered home ownership either?

States also have "targeted areas" where the first-time home-buyer requirement is completely waived in order to promote home ownership in that area. Targeted areas also allow higher household income when borrowers are trying to qualify.

Another exception to the first-time homebuyer rule can be single parents. If a single parent has custody of minor children for at least six months out of the year, they may be able to utilize their state housing program even if they've owned a home in the last three years.

Utah recently gave veterans a blanket exception to the first-time homebuyer requirement. Any veteran using a VA loan who can comply with the income and sales price limits can use our state housing program. They can also use the closing cost assistance program. This means a veteran can do a VA loan (that is limited to 100% of the purchase price) with a small second mortgage granted by Utah Housing to cover their closing costs. They are getting 103% financing, purchasing a home with no money, and doing it without any concessions from Realtors or sellers. Tell me that isn't a great deal for everybody!

DOES MY BUYER NEED A SPECIAL HOMEBUYER EDUCATION CLASS?

That depends. Some states require the class; some have dropped this requirement. The class has excellent information but was also considered by many as "just another government hoop."

WHAT KIND OF LOANS ARE MY BUYERS GETTING?

Once again, that depends. In Utah, FHA or VA loans are the only loan types used. A buyer simply qualifies for one or the other and the loan is funded by Utah Housing at their current below-market interest rate. Utah Housing then services the loan. Many states offer conventional loans as well.

FHA loans are commonly used because of their more relaxed credit standards and debt-to-income ratio guidelines. Many first-time homebuyers need that extra flexibility. Review Chapter 8 if you want to aggressively advocate your state's housing program. You'll probably be working with a lot of FHA financing.

CAN MY BUYER RENT OUT A HOME FINANCED WITH STATE HOUSING?

Usually, no. These programs are not designed to help investors acquire income properties. They are designed to provide home ownership opportunities to buyers within the prescribed income limits. I do know that some states will work with buyers and grant permission to rent a property under certain circumstances. I also know that states reserve the right to call the loan due if an owner is renting the property without permission from the agency.

WHAT ABOUT CO-SIGNERS?

Non-occupying co-signers are allowed under some programs (FHA, for example). The typical scenario is Mom or Dad co-signs with Junior to buy his first home. You will probably find that the state housing program has its own restrictive guidelines on co-signers regarding an allowable debt-to-income ratio. Here in Utah it's 40%. That means that Mom and Dad's total debt ratio, including Junior's new house payment, can't exceed 40% of their gross income.

A common misconception regarding co-signers is that as long as they are good enough, you'll get the loan. I've had many loan applicants with well-to-do parents quickly lose their smirk when I unloaded this little bit of data at their feet. They assumed that with Daddy co-signing, the loan was "in the bag."

The reality is that good credit doesn't erase bad. A co-signer is for qualifying income assistance only. All borrowers must still have acceptable credit. Speaking of which, here in Utah, our state housing program has a mid credit score requirement on all borrowers of 620 (unless no credit scores are present). This means that when we pull a three credit bureau report, two of the three scores must be 620 or higher on all borrowers. If there are no scores for borrowers, we must try to provide alternative sources of credit (i.e., verification of rent, utilities, etc.) and analyze the borrower's worthiness that way. Check with your state to see if they have similar restrictions.

WHAT IS RECAPTURE?

Recapture is an IRS tax penalty. This rule can come into play on state housing loans when a buyer sells a home. The rule was created to try to "recapture" tax funds that the government missed out on because this loan was funded through the sale of tax-free bonds.

In true government fashion, the penalty is a convoluted calculation that says *if* you sell your home in the first nine years of ownership, and *if* you make a certain amount of profit, and *if* your income has risen to a certain level at the time you sell, you *may* owe the IRS some money.

It's important to note here that very few people ever have to pay the recapture tax penalty. However, lenders use this penalty constantly as a scare tactic to talk buyers out of doing state housing loans. Why? Two reasons:

1. They aren't approved to do state housing loans and they don't want to lose the client to a lender who is, or;

2. They can do a state housing loan but don't want to because the profit margin is so much smaller.

There, I said it. Here you are working so hard to help this wide-eyed, newly married couple move in to their first home and create a "client for life" while their lender of choice is trying to railroad them into a larger house payment with a higher interest rate so he can make the payment on his Jaguar that month. Lenders: We can be a seedy bunch.

Utah was so frustrated with this whole "scare tactic" business that they developed the policy that any borrower who had to pay recapture tax would be reimbursed by Utah Housing, effectively eliminating the recapture tax and the scare tactic. Utah recognized the rarity of this penalty, so they put their own money on the line.

But thank goodness this couple found you! You are going to ask a few questions, find out what Loser Lending was trying to do to them, and offer them names of great lenders you know who will help them explore the state housing program.

DON'T THESE PROGRAMS RUN OUT OF MONEY?

This has always been a main sticking point with state housing loans. The money for these loans comes from the sale of bonds. When the money ran out, buyers, sellers, loan officers, and Realtors would be on hold until a new bond issue came out and there was money again. This can be disastrous for your transaction as well as contingent closings before and after this one. You can't blame anyone for shying away from this potential snafu.

Recent changes in some states have ended this glitch. They now have systems in place that allow for continuous flow of funds. It works and it is heaven! Hopefully your state is one that has made the change or may have it coming in the near future.

Use your state housing loan programs to their fullest to serve your buyers and sellers. Work with a lender to help you make state housing flyers for your listings that fall within the parameters. Nothing is more powerful than a flyer that clearly advertises a house payment and a legitimate, low-interest, no money out-of-pocket program. (Be sure your lender is Truth-in-Lending compliant in their advertising.) The reality check of numbers in black and white can encourage potential qualified homebuyers and discourage buyers who are just looking and don't have a good grasp on the true monthly cost of owning a home. This saves everybody time and money and that's what I'm all about helping you to do!

C H A P T E R   1 0

HUD Homes: Guiding Your Bargain Hunters

William is a hard-working guy who is always on the lookout for a deal. He has fair credit and he is the perfect state housing program buyer. Combine his credit with no money for down payment or closing costs and he is definitely an FHA borrower. William has come to you with the announcement: "I want to buy a HUD home. They're FHA foreclosures, right? I'm not afraid of a place that needs some fix-up; I just want to get it for a good price."

You have registered with the company that manages HUD homes in your state, but this will be your first transaction. So you and William start trolling online to find that perfect HUD property. On day four of the search, you call William early one morning to say, "I've found a great one. It was just listed this morning. Let's go take a look."

William loves it, so you go back to the office to place the online offer. The price on this property is very reasonable and William really wants it. You've looked at the area market and know that the home is worth at least $10,000 more than the asking price. You explain to him that other offers will be going into HUD on the same property and you'll have to wait to see who wins the bid.

"You mean it's not first come, first served?" he asks, bewildered.

"No. HUD looks at all of the bids during a certain time frame and selects a winner," you explain.

"Well, I really want the home and you said that it is worth more than they are asking. Since I qualify for more than the sales price, can't I just bid over the sales price to give me a better chance of winning the bid?"

This seems like a good strategy, so you enter William's bid for $10,000 over the sales price. After all, he is pre-approved with a reputable lender for more than this bid. Two days later you are notified that William won the bid. He is thrilled and you have just set him up for a big disappointment: He will have to pay the extra $10,000 out of his own pocket.

HUD homes are priced from value information received on a new FHA appraisal that occurs when the home is being readied for sale. This FHA appraisal is valid for six months and lenders are required to use it with any FHA loan on this property.

So let's say that HUD listed this property for $120,000. Most likely, the existing FHA appraisal on this home shows the value at $120,000. If I am William's lender, I cannot calculate a loan amount from the accepted bid price of $130,000. I must use the appraised value of $120,000, which means that the only way William is going to purchase this home is if he can bring in the $10,000 difference in cash.

If William could qualify under a conventional loan program, a lender would be allowed to do a new appraisal in conjunction with the loan. If the new appraisal showed a value of $130,000 or more, the problem would be solved.

DEALING WITH THE RED TAPE

HUD homes do offer great bargain opportunities for your clients, but like any other specialty situation, you have to know the process. This next true-life hiccup, as in deal-killing hiccup, happened to a client of mine. It wasn't really avoidable, but it will give you some insight into the never-ending fun of government red tape.

Keith and Jane won a bid on a HUD home. It was a one-in-a-million find. Good neighborhood, great price, excellent condition. Keith and Jane were also FHA first-time homebuyers. Our loan file was very complete and we were going to be able to use the existing FHA appraisal on the property. This translates to "very fast closing." They were so excited. They were living in a two-bedroom apartment with three lively children. They needed the space. They needed to move. They needed it now.

I was familiar with HUD transactions and was looking forward to my fastest HUD closing yet. My file was ready for final underwriting within three days of receiving a finalized contract from HUD. All I needed was my title report.

I called the title company repeatedly over the next few days. Each day I was told, "It's coming." Normally, title reports are created very quickly on these properties. HUD's marketing and management contractors require that certain title and escrow companies to handle their transactions. Two weeks later, it was finally disclosed to me that the process of putting the Office of Housing and Urban Development back on title as the owner was not complete. The attorneys were working on it.

Okay, this warrants the question, "How can HUD sell a property it doesn't even own yet?" I still to this day do not understand how it happened. All I know is that my borrowers were tapping their toes waiting to close.

This sales contract set a 45-day deadline for closing from the date of contract acceptance. We were coming up on the deadline. Finally, I get my title report and we were ready to close.

I'm going to talk more about the unique HUD settlement process later, but for now just know that things work a little different. HUD requires their side of the transaction to be signed and accepted first before they will allow the buyer to sign. So we send off documents to the escrow company, which sends them to HUD. We're allowed to schedule settlement for my buyer the next week—Monday, to be exact. As long as HUD accepts the documents and settlement statement we are good to go. Finally, we are almost home free! It's three weeks later than we should have closed, but at least it's finally happening. Or so I thought.

On Friday afternoon at 4:50 p.m., my phone rings. It's Jane. She's crying. Keith has just been laid off from his job. The employer says that the layoff is temporary, only 30 days. But they won't guarantee it. The loan is now dead unless my borrower gets a new job before Monday. We are at the end of the deadline on the contract. An extension is possible, but my clients choose not to pursue it.

The good news is that Keith was re-hired after 35 days and still works for the same company. They had enough savings to see them through the 35 days, and had they closed when we had their loan ready, they would be in their new home right now. Lesson learned: Be prepared for anything and don't assume HUD always has their act together.

Here's another quick fact about HUD homes: First-round bids must be for primary residence buyers. Investment property and second-home bids will be considered in a subsequent bidding round.

HELPING YOUR BUYER

In most transactions, a competent lender is key to a smooth settlement. In a HUD home transaction, you and your buyer are in big trouble without one. There will be some abrupt and unwelcome surprises if a lender isn't familiar with the way HUD works. If you find yourself doubting the experience level of a lender involved with your buyer, here are some key points that will help you guide your buyer and ask the right questions of the lender to prompt the necessary action and meet the contract deadline.

- HUD does not automatically provide title insurance for your buyer. Most buyers want an owner's policy. Make sure your buyer is aware that this cost, which can be substantial, will be deferred to them. An inexperienced lender may not include this in your buyer's good faith estimate. In your bid, you may ask HUD to pay up to 3% of the sales price toward your buyer's settlement costs, and this money could be used to cover an owner's policy for your client.

- Escrow companies require documents be delivered to them well in advance of the actual settlement. Requirements vary, but it's usually between five and ten days.

- HUD requires that the documents and settlement statement be accepted by their representatives *before* a buyer is allowed to sign.

- HUD requires that the loan funds be received by the title company *before* a buyer is allowed to sign.

These requirements can pose some major problems to a lender who doesn't have the in-house ability for early document and funds delivery. A mortgage broker, for instance, usually doesn't underwrite their own files, print their own documents, or wire loan funds. For those procedures, they are at the mercy of the lender they have brokered the file to.

Probe the lender for details on these processes and specifically ask if this has been done before successfully. Better to
change lenders mid-stream than have your buyer lose the
home.

Keep this information close at hand for your next buyer
who is a HUD bargain hunter. Your client will be glad you
did!

CHAPTER 11

VA Loans: Well Worth Learning the Ins and Outs

In 1944, Congress passed the Serviceman's Readjustment Act, more commonly known as the GI Bill. As part of the bill, the Department of Veterans Affairs Loan Guaranty Program was established.

Veterans Affairs (VA) loans are another financing tool for any of your buyers who are eligible veterans or spouses of deceased veterans. These loans are similar to FHA loans in a lot of respects. For example, VA does not actually make loans; it insures or "guarantees" the loans made by lenders under VA guidelines. VA also has property standard requirements that are part of the appraisal process. Unfortunately, VA has not followed FHA's lead on relaxing those standards.

Since September 11, the number of borrowers eligible for VA loans has increased dramatically, primarily due to deployment of Reserve and National Guard units. These soldiers would normally have a six-year service requirement before they were eligible for a VA loan. Because of active-duty deployment, many meet the 90 continuous days of wartime service requirement and are now eligible way ahead of the normal schedule. This means it is much more likely that you will be working with veteran buyers who choose VA financing.

VA LOAN BASICS

Here are some basics about the program that make it so attractive to veterans:

- 100% financing (all under one low, fixed-interest-rate first mortgage)

- 100% financing for loan amounts up to $417,000 on a single-family home (higher in Hawaii, Alaska, Guam, and Virgin Islands)

- Relaxed credit standards

- No pre-payment penalties

- No monthly mortgage insurance

- Loans are assumable by veterans and non-veterans alike

- Sellers can pay up to 4% in sales concessions to buyers in addition to closing costs and discount points (pre-paid and escrow items must be included in the 4% calculation)

- Seller can pay off debt for buyer (yes, it's true)

The absence of monthly mortgage insurance makes a big difference in a monthly payment. When I start comparing 100% fixed-rate financing options with applicants, it's impossible to beat a VA monthly payment.

VA does charge a "funding fee" on each loan, which is paid directly to VA. This fee can be, and usually is, added to the loan amount. This is how VA is able to have funds available to pay losses on guaranteed loans. The fee schedule on a 100% financing purchase loan works like this:

Veteran Type	First-Time Use Percentage	Subsequent Use Percentage
Regular Military	2.15%	3.3%
National Guard / Reserves	2.40%	3.3%
Disabled Veterans	Waived	Waived

Reduced funding fees apply when the borrower has 5% or 10% down, but the most common purchase scenario is 100% financing with no down payment.

As I stated in a previous chapter, most states will let a veteran first-time homebuyer use state housing program money, making their interest rate and payment even lower. Some even waive the first-time homebuyer restriction.

I cannot stress enough how important it is that your buyer have a knowledgeable VA lender, specifically one who is an automatic lender and is LAPP (Lender Appraisal Processing Program) approved. These lenders have full authority and control over the loan and can speed the process considerably. Lenders who are not "automatic" and LAPP-approved have to rely upon their regional VA offices for assistance with loan review and issuance of the Notice of Value once the appraisal has been completed.

A good VA lender will process your veteran buyer's loan just as quickly as a conventional loan and make it look easy. An inexperienced lender will make your life and your buyer's miserable, because a VA loan is easy only if you know exactly what you are doing.

Here's some more good information you can pass along to the veteran buyer who has all the finance questions for you at your Saturday open house.

VERIFYING ELIGIBILITY

The first step to obtaining a VA loan is to get your Certificate of Eligibility (COE). This is the document that verifies that this borrower is, in fact, eligible for a VA loan. Alternatively, this document may show another mortgage currently "tying up" the eligibility. If this existing mortgage can't or won't be paid in full before or concurrent with the purchase of the new home, then a VA loan won't be possible.

This situation might happen if a veteran had purchased a previous home using their VA eligibility, still owned the home, and hadn't paid off the mortgage. This is quite common when veterans decide to keep a home and rent it out after purchasing it with a VA loan. It's also possible that a home was sold, but the veteran allowed the buyer to assume his VA loan. If the buyer was not a veteran or was a veteran but didn't substitute his own VA eligibility to replace the existing veteran's eligibility, the original eligibility is still "tied up" with this mortgage.

Speaking of loan assumptions, there is some critical information you will want to pass on to a seller who is considering allowing a buyer to assume his current VA loan. If the assuming buyer can't (because they aren't an eligible veteran) or won't be substituting their own eligibility for your seller's, notify the seller of this fact:

> *If a buyer defaults on the loan, VA will not hold your seller financially responsible. (That's the good news.) VA also will not restore your seller's eligibility—ever. (That's the part that stinks.)*

This could be an important consideration when a seller is contemplating the best course of action. VA financing might come in handy later on down the road. Just be sure your seller is aware of this rule.

Okay, let's get back to the Certificate of Eligibility. The easiest way to obtain a COE is to have the buyers visit Ms. Super Competent VA Automatic LAPP–Approved Lender who can order the document electronically for them. In some cases, the COE will be provided instantly online. Worst case, they will need to provide a proof-of-service document, the most common being a DD-214 Certificate of Release or Discharge from Active Duty, which the super competent lender will know how to scan and upload to the VA Eligibility Center along with an online Request for Certificate of Eligibility. The VA Eligibility Center will be able to email the COE to the lender within two weeks or notify the lender of any additional information they need to complete the process.

RESTORING ELIGIBILITY

The rules regarding VA loan eligibility, and specifically the restoration of that eligibility if it's been used previously, can really throw a monkey wrench into your transaction. For all of the reasons listed earlier, I love VA loans and I feel good about providing them to my borrowers whenever possible. However, I do want to give you a few more pointers on recognizing some little known circumstances regarding restoration of eligibility that may take a VA loan option out of the picture for your buyers.

Brent and Sheila had purchased their first home with a VA loan 25 years ago. They lived there for 15 years. During that time Sheila received a small inheritance from her grandmother and they paid the mortgage in full.

A job transfer moved them to another state. They decided to keep their current home and rent it out, hoping one day to return and retire there. They purchased a new home in their new state, using VA financing again. Ten years later, Brent's employer asked him to relocate once more. Due to a downturn in the real estate market, they were lucky to sell the home, pay the Realtor, pay off the mortgage, and still walk away with a few thousand dollars. Health challenges and medical bills had bruised their credit and depleted their savings a few years earlier.

After meeting with a lender in their new city, it was determined that if they wanted to do 100% financing, VA was their best bet. Their lender submitted the electronic application for a new Certificate of Eligibility. Two weeks later the lender received notice that Brent would not be granted restoration of his eligibility.

The lender never saw this problem coming. Why? Because the loan application reflected one investment property owned free and clear and one primary residence recently sold with a VA mortgage paid-in-full. What was there to be concerned about? The previous VA loan was paid off, which should have cleared the eligibility, right?

Wrong. The problem here lies with Brent and Sheila's first home. VA allows a one-time-only restoration of eligibility when a property financed with VA is retained. A lender would have had to know this specific restriction and asked the question regarding the original loan on their investment property in order to detect this issue.

The lesson here for you, the Realtor, is if you have a potential VA borrower and they mention another property that they own, inquire if the property was purchased using a VA loan. If they say yes, remind them to mention this to the lender. It could indicate a potential problem that is best uncovered now so alternative financing can be considered.

ALIVE AND WELL LETTERS

In Chapter 1, I mentioned that, since September 11, it has become common to use a power-of-attorney with VA loans due to veteran deployment. Another caveat with a VA loan is that if a veteran is deployed to a war zone and a power-of-attorney is used, the lender must obtain an alive and well letter from a commanding officer, indicating that the individual is, in fact, alive and well.

The veteran's spouse will have contact information to reach the necessary parties to obtain this letter, but an inexperienced lender could hold up a settlement if they aren't aware of this requirement. The loan officer will find out (usually right before settlement) from the underwriter, and will start scrambling to get this condition met. A simple inquiry from you during loan processing along the lines of, "So how are you coming with that alive and well letter?" could be the right question at the right time to avoid delays. Once again, your knowledge will help save the deal—or at least keep it moving along.

Right about now you might be thinking, "How likely is this power-of-attorney stuff? My gosh, this would mean that spouses are buying houses that their veteran husbands or wives haven't even seen yet. That doesn't seem too likely to me."

You'd be surprised. Realtors and lenders are seeing this happen more and more. The biggest reason? The Internet. Many deployed soldiers have Internet access and can see information, view pictures, and take virtual tours. Their comfort level is heightened considerably when faced with placing all of the home purchase control with a spouse.

REPAIR ISSUES

When you are listing a property, it's a great idea to screen the home for repair issues that could be addressed ahead of time to widen the pool of prospective buyers to include those who prefer to use VA financing.

I've seen many homes listed on the MLS that state the standard language: "Financing Options—Cash, conventional, FHA, VA." Don't throw in the standard language unless you've done some screening! You can't guarantee a seller that a VA appraiser won't find a repair issue, but a little pre-listing work could help alleviate problems later on or notify a seller of possible repair requirements if an offer is made that includes a VA loan. It can also clarify a seller's adamant intent that the home be sold "as is" with no sales concessions for repairs. Better you find out now about the inflexibility of that seller.

Here are the most common items you will want to screen for:

- Handrails (all stairs containing three or more risers need a handrail)

- Cracked or damaged exit doors

- Defective paint surfaces (chipped or peeling paint on

interior or exterior of home; exposed exterior wood protected with paint or stain)

- Termites (inspection and/or treatment required if home has wood to ground contact, infestation exists, or home is located in a moderate to heavy probability for infestation area [see map at www.agoodinspector.com/termite_map.htm])

- Private septic systems (may need inspection if area is known for soil percolation problems, local authority requires it, or underwriter requires it)

- Private wells require water inspection

- Damaged walls or ceilings

- Trip hazards (sink holes in concrete, poorly installed carpet)

- Crawl spaces (no debris or trash, must be adequate access, must be adequate space for maintenance of plumbing and ductwork, no pooling of water or excessive dampness)

- Inadequate access/egress from bedrooms to exterior of home

- Leaking or worn out roof

- Flat roof requires a roof inspection

- Evidence of structural problems

- Faulty or defective mechanical systems (electrical, plumbing, heating)

- Streets must have an all-weather surface

- High voltage electric lines (property cannot be located within the transmission line easement)

- Flood zone (property cannot be located in flood hazard area where flood insurance is not available)

- Noise (property cannot be located in a high noise airport zone)

- Condo or PUD (Is project approved by VA or FHA?)

This list will help you screen for the most common minimum property requirements that can require mandatory repairs for a VA loan. Use this list to help you screen properties for your VA buyers as well.

Remember, too, that once your listing has had a VA appraisal done, that appraisal (or rather the final Notice of Value) and the corresponding case number are attached to that property for six months. If a VA buyer's loan falls through and you get another offer from a VA buyer within six months, the existing appraisal stands and must be used for a VA loan. The only rare exception is in areas of major market volatility. Occasionally, the argument could be made to allow a new appraisal, but again, the exception is rare.

UNMARRIED COUPLES

Here's another illusory VA loan fact that you can impress your clients with: If a veteran and non-veteran are purchasing a home together and are not married, the veteran is limited to only one half of his/her entitlement.

I recently helped David and Kim, an unmarried couple, purchase their new home. David is currently enlisted in the Air Force and Kim works in a civilian position on the military base where David is stationed. Kim is not a veteran.

Due to past credit problems and no down payment, VA financing was their best option, especially when combined with their state housing program. Unfortunately, because they weren't married and the home they were trying to purchase had a sales price of $225,000 (more than one half of the $417,000 limit for 100% financing) we couldn't do a VA loan. They were able to secure a state housing loan, but their monthly payment was slightly higher.

SELLER PAYING OFF BUYERS' DEBT

Remember how I told you at the start of this chapter that one of the good things about VA loans for buyers is that the seller can pay off their debt? The tights and cape can come out now, because you are about to save the deal in a big way. This is definitely some outstanding knowledge and here's how one couple benefited from it.

Peggy and Don found the perfect home. They had run through some numbers and were a little concerned because they knew that their debt-to-income ratio was a little high. And like many first-time homebuyers they needed 100% financing. They needed to get to a loan officer quickly so they could get pre-approved.

Enter Mr. Super Competent Automatic VA LAPP–Approved Lender. After taking their application and confirming their fear that, yes, their debt-to-income ratio was too high for loan approval, he offered a solution.

Peggy and Don had a $250 monthly car payment. They only owed $3500 on the car. Mr. Lender explained that if that debt was eliminated they would qualify for the home.

"But we don't have the money to pay off the car," they replied.

"You don't need the money. The seller can pay the debt for you." He then walked them through the numbers.

The home had a sales price of $200,000. VA allows a seller to pay up to 4% in sales concessions in addition to closing costs. This translates into a maximum of $8,000 in sales concessions, plus closing costs. Don and Peggy had no money for closing costs or pre-paid items as well. It was determined that their needs were the following:

- Seller to pay $3500 to eliminate buyer's car loan

- Seller to pay $1000 toward buyer's pre-paid/escrow items

- Seller to pay $3000 toward buyer's closing costs

Two days later they had an accepted offer.

Granted this will not work for every seller or every property, but it is a valuable, unique twist to VA loans that most Realtors, lenders, and borrowers have no idea exists. But you, the savvy Realtor, will be ready with this tidbit of information along with all of the other VA financing facts to enlighten a less-than-expert loan officer, impress a client, and smooth the way for your transaction. I'll say it again: baby-sit, baby-sit, baby-sit. Your check could depend on it.

WORD OF WARNING

Do you know what happens to your commission when your VA buyer decides to buy a For Sale By Owner (FSBO) property?

"Why, Tracey," you say, "my buyer has signed a buyer's agency agreement with me, so I'll be paid either by the seller or my buyer, just like any other FSBO transaction that I represent a buyer in."

No, you won't. If the seller refuses to pay a commission, you cannot charge a commission or any related fees for your services to a veteran buyer. Keep this in mind so you don't learn this one the hard way—as in, right at settlement when a lender reviews the settlement statement and you get the news that your buyer representation was just performed for free. Ouch!

CHAPTER 1 2

Flood Zones: Crossing Muddy Waters

Is this property located in a flood zone? That is always the bottom line any Realtor wants to know—both for disclosure on a listing and in determining a property's attributes for a buyer's consideration. If it is, flood insurance will be required by the mortgage guidelines. As a lender, I can tell you that this is the exact same question, stated in the same terms, that we ask when processing a loan file. Well, what if I told you that while this is always the question asked, it's the wrong one?

We are going to need some background to sort this out.

This chapter will be received in many different ways by Realtors, depending on their geographic areas. Those Realtors constantly dealing with properties that require flood insurance are probably better informed on the intricacies of flood zones than those of us in states where floods are random and unexpected. Our flood issues are about snow melt and sudden storms, not hurricanes or days of constant rainfall. Whatever group you're in, I hope you learn something new.

First off, *every* property is located in a flood zone. The question should be: Is this property located in a high-risk flood zone? Now let's take a closer look at some flood zone facts.

DETERMINING RISK

The Federal Emergency Management Agency (FEMA) creates maps referred to as Flood Hazard Boundary Maps or Flood Insurance Rate Maps (FIRM). These maps designate areas to be in one of two overall zones—either moderate- to low-risk, or high-risk. Within these two categories exists different zone designations.

Risk Level	*Flood Hazard Zone*
Moderate- to Low-Risk Area	Zones B, C, & X (No flood insurance required)
High-Risk Area	Zones A, AE, A1–A30, AH, AO, AR, A99, V, VE, V1–30 (Flood insurance required)

You can refer to Appendix D for FEMA's zone code definitions.

The only exception to the required flood insurance in a high-risk area would be the rare occasion when a mortgage was not made under the guidelines of FHA, VA, Rural Housing, Fannie Mae, or Freddie Mac. In other words, a private lender was holding and servicing the note with no intention of selling the loan. However, it makes no sense for a homeowner to own a property in a high-risk flood zone without proper coverage.

So, you are listing a property and you want to know if the property is in a high-risk flood zone. The obvious first step is to ask the seller. Don't ever assume that a property is not in a high-risk area; areas can vary from one house to another. Just because the house across the street that you listed last year was low risk doesn't mean this home will be. Streams, drainage areas, and elevations can differ greatly over a very short distance.

I've seen several deals fall apart when it was discovered that a property was in a high-risk zone after the offer was accepted and we had started the loan process. I honestly don't know in these cases if it was the seller, the Realtor, or both who decided to leave out that little detail in the disclosures, but in every case the buyer walked. Besides the legal and ethical issues at hand, you will never win by crossing your fingers and hoping for the best. Critical omissions cast a shadow on a transaction. It is my personal policy to order a flood certification on a loan file at the beginning of the process, saving the borrowers involved the expense of an appraisal, if they choose to cancel the contract due to the unexpected news that this home will require flood insurance.

I've also experienced a situation where an entire new subdivision was originally determined to be in a high-risk flood zone, but had obtained a Letter of Map Revision from FEMA changing the zone. Of course, this was wonderful news. However, the Realtor, who was representing both builder and buyer, didn't bother to notify anyone of this until our loan processing produced a flood certification showing the property in a high-risk zone. We notified the buyer, who immediately called the Realtor, who faxed us the letter. We then sent the letter to our flood certificate service provider and all was well, but not before a few frustrating moments were had by all.

You may be wondering why the flood certificate service provider wasn't aware of this change. I certainly was. Upon calling them, they explained to me that the flood plain maps are changing constantly. It is their company policy to get updated data from FEMA every six months. Obviously, this particular change had happened since their last update. Had this loan been processed a few months later, I would have been spared a gray hair or two.

It's also possible for you to check on flood risk at www.floodsmart.gov. Click on "What's Your Flood Risk?" for a relative determination of risk. Exact determination will be researched by both the lender and the appraiser. This online tool is great, but many areas are not available for online lookup yet. If your area isn't, keep checking back. FEMA is updating these maps constantly to make them digitally available to the public under their Flood Map Modernization program.

As FEMA works through their Map Modernization program, some communities will have significant changes. Zone determinations may change, which will be good news for some and bad news for others. When a homebuyer signs his or her mortgage papers, there is a document that states that they will agree to obtain flood coverage at any time that the property is determined to be in a high-risk flood zone.

RAISING CLIENT AWARENESS

As a Realtor, if you are involved in a community that is undergoing proposed changes to its maps, here are some great ideas on how to raise awareness by providing past clients and all their neighbors with this helpful information. It's a great public service and wonderful marketing tool.

- Notify households of the possible changes. Flyers may be a good option.

- Check with county or city offices so you can provide information on websites to view new proposed maps, dates for public comment and appeals, and date of final map adoption.

- Give out this link—http://www.fema.gov/plan/prevent/fhm/hm_main.shtm—to obtain forms and information on how to request a zone change for their property.

- Advise homeowners who are facing change to a high-risk zone that they may get better rates if they purchase their flood insurance now, before the new map is adopted. A process known as "grandfathering" may allow them to keep their lower risk premium after the zone change. They should consult an insurance agent immediately as it takes 30 days for a flood policy to go into effect, unless it's purchased as a requirement for a mortgage.

With all this talk of flood insurance, we'd better explore what it is, how to get it, and why a homeowner would want it.

FLOOD INSURANCE

The National Flood Insurance Program (NFIP) is a federal program that allows property owners to purchase insurance against losses from flooding. Regular homeowners' policies do not cover losses from flooding. Floods are defined as overflow from inland or tidal waters, runoff of surface waters, mudflow, and collapse of land along the shore of a lake or other body of water; it does not cover those occasions when the hose to your washing machine bursts and floods your basement. (A homeowner's policy should take care of that one.)

The Flood Disaster Protection Act of 1973 made the purchase of flood insurance mandatory on properties located in high-risk flood zones. This insurance can be purchased through the NFIP if the property lies in a community that chooses to participate in the NFIP. To see if your community participates in the NFIP go to www.fema.gov/fema/csb.shtm.

If a community chooses not to participate within one year after a high-risk flood hazard has been mapped, flood insurance and federal financial assistance will not be available under the NFIP for the purchase or construction of a home in a high-risk area.

Also, if a presidentially declared natural disaster happens due to flooding in a nonparticipating community, no federal financial assistance can be provided for the permanent repair or reconstruction of buildings in these areas. It is, however, possible for a community to apply and be accepted into the NFIP within six months of a presidential disaster declaration and have the limitations on federal assistance lifted.

Most homeowners incorrectly assume that if their home floods, federal disaster assistance will pay for their damages. Federal disaster assistance only offers interest-bearing loans to help cover flood damage, and only if the President declares the area a disaster. Fewer than 10 percent of all weather emergencies in the United States become declared disaster areas.

WHAT DOES A FLOOD POLICY COVER?

A standard flood policy will cover:

- Structural damage

- Furnace, water heater, and air conditioner

- Flood debris cleanup

- Floor surfaces such as carpeting and tile

Additional coverage can be purchased to cover the contents of your home, and most insurance companies offer excess flood coverage to provide additional structure coverage beyond the limits of a dwelling (most homes) or residential condominium building association (condos) flood policy.

I hope this information will help you stand out from the competition as you work to represent sellers and buyers using your first-class method of customer service. It can be tough putting a positive spin on a property that requires flood insurance when it's in an area where high-risk zones are the exception to the rule. Maybe extra disclosure on flood insurance premiums and advertising "no flood loss in 20 years" (if that's the case) could help ease prospective buyers' minds as they consider this listing. Maybe the premiums aren't as high as a buyer would have guessed. And perhaps the facts you can offer about flood insurance will provide a degree of comfort that might offset the negative aspect of purchasing a home that requires flood insurance.

Knowledge is power, so use these lessons to your advantage.

CHAPTER 13

Risk Underwriting and Mortgage Loans

When you list a property, it's a pretty one-dimensional picture. I'm not saying it's easy, I'm just saying that in most cases, it is what it is. There are not a lot of variables to deal with as far as the property itself. A brick rambler on .25 acres with three bedrooms, two and a half baths, and a two-car garage in a great family neighborhood is the product you are selling. Or maybe you've got a one-bedroom, one-bath condo in a resort area. Unless you've got a cash buyer, it's the financing of the property that usually complicates your job.

Why does it have to be that way? You've got a seller with a property and a buyer who wants it. What is the problem? Two words: risk underwriting.

For the purpose of mortgage loans, risk underwriting is the process of analyzing the loan's overall risk and determining if it is within an acceptable range. In other words, the lender is trying to make loans that have a low chance of default. Any loan being evaluated is assessed using the performance history data of millions of past mortgage loans. Risk assessment is the driving force behind the actual underwriting of the transaction.

Automated underwriting programs evaluate a loan application and apply risk underwriting to determine an underwriting recommendation. The use of automated software allows for much faster changes to risk assessment as cumulative loan performance data is gathered and trends identified. Underwriting guidelines can be made more or less restrictive on as specific or broad an application as necessary.

Let me explain all these factors and then we'll examine situations and give you some insight on why or why not a deal will go through and how you can offer helpful advice to those new buyers you're hoping to represent.

RISK FACTORS

There are two categories of risk: primary and secondary. Primary risk is all about the borrower, and only two questions really matter:

- How much down payment does the borrower have?

- What is the borrower's credit history?

Historically, the default risk drops as the amount of down payment goes up. And, as you'd suspect, the better the past credit history, the less chance of default.

Secondary risk looks at all of the other factors of the file.

- *Liquid Reserves:* Money in the bank, investments, retirement funds, etc. The higher the reserves, the lower the default probability.

- *Debt-to-Income Ratio:* Very low debt ratios tend to have low default rates while very high ratios are just the opposite.

- *Transaction Type:* Purchase transactions are lower risk than refinance loans; the greater the loan increase on a refinance, the higher the default risk.

- *Employment Type:* Salaried/hourly wage earners have lower default rates than self-employed borrowers.

- *Mortgage Term:* Data shows that fixed-rate mortgages with a term less than 30 years perform better.

- *Loan Type:* Adjustable rate and balloon mortgages have higher default rates than loans with fixed payments.

- *Property Type:* Single-family detached homes have a

much lower default rate than a three- or four-unit property.

- *Co-Borrowers:* Mortgages with two or more borrowers tend to perform better than mortgages with one borrower.

- *Previous Late Mortgage Payments:* Past mortgage payment history is a strong factor in the overall credit history in predicting future default risk. In other words, a late payment on a credit card is not nearly as negative an influence on risk assessment as a late mortgage payment.

- *Prior Bankruptcy or Foreclosure:* The presence of either one of these indicates a much higher default potential.

Automated underwriting programs look at the primary and secondary risk factors and then determine if the overall risk is acceptable. Certain loan products allow a higher threshold of risk when specific criteria are met. A good example is loan products that have been specifically designed to benefit low-to-moderate income borrowers who are purchasing a primary residence. These loan products tolerate higher risk levels in order for the goal of better serving the low-to-moderate income borrower to be achieved.

Okay, now that you know a little more about risk factors let's see if we can translate this into some information that you can share, once again, at that Saturday open house with those finance-curious clients that are bound to show up.

CREDIT HISTORY

Because credit history and credit scores are a primary risk factor and the source of so much mystery, we'll start there.

Roger and Penny have come to your open house because this little starter home would be perfect for them. But like many first-time homebuyers, they are intimidated by the loan process. They both have good salaries, but they are unsure of their current and past credit status. After chatting for a few minutes, they begin asking you questions. Here are some of the more common ones you should be prepared to answer:

Q. Should we just go to a lender and have them pull our credit report or should we get one on our own first?

A. Ideally, you should get your report on your own first to be sure of what's there and have the opportunity to work on any problems that you find. You can go to each of the credit bureaus individually and get a report, or obtain a consolidated report of all three bureaus combined. The three bureaus are TransUnion (www.transunion.com), Equifax (www.equifax.com), and Experian (www.experian.com). It's very important to review the information from all three bureaus since every creditor does not report to every bureau, so data will vary.

Q. What if we find something wrong on the report?

A. All three bureaus can be contacted regarding disputes/ investigations either online, by mail, or by phone. Contact information is available at their websites.

Q. How long will it take to fix an incorrect item?

A. Simple corrections that have accompanying documentation can be fixed within a few days. Investigations regarding loan fraud and/or identity theft can be a much longer process.

Q. We want our credit score to be as high as possible. What can we do to improve it?

A. Here are the main things you can do to improve your credit score and keep it high:

- *Pay your accounts on time.* Late payments, especially those occurring within the last 12 months, can have a significant impact on your score.

- *Don't apply for new credit too often.* When you apply for new credit, the company you applied with does an inquiry to look at your report. That inquiry becomes part of your permanent credit history. Too many inquiries can negatively impact your score. Shopping for a new car and applying for a car loan several different places over a six-week period is a great example of what *not* to do right before you try to qualify for a mortgage.

- *Keep credit card balances low.* One of the best ways to improve a score is to pay down revolving balances. Keeping credit cards paid off or below 30% of the available balance is the key. I've had clients experience 10–80 point improvements in scores just by paying down their credit cards.

- *Old credit is good credit.* Don't get in too big of a hurry to close old inactive accounts with a good payment history. That account might be helping to keep your score up.

- *Do not rush to pay off collection accounts until you've talked with a lender.* This seems like crazy advice, but there's a good reason. It's important that you pay your obligations; however, timing can be everything. Let's say you have a $1700 collection account that is 13 months old. It has not been updated to the bureaus since it was initially reported. Believe it or not, paying the collection account will temporarily lower your score because the item will be updated when you pay it, giving that negative item and its impact a more recent date and a larger influence over your score. While this account may still have to be paid in order to approve your mortgage loan, a lender may advise you to pay it at closing.

Q. If we paid off all of our credit cards, how long will it take for our scores to improve?

A. It will usually take at least 30–45 days for the credit card companies to update the bureaus regarding your new balance. Your lender will have access to special "Rapid Rescore" services that can, for a fee, request a bureau to update a certain account immediately and then "rescore" your credit based on that new information. This process can usually be done within a week. This is an especially powerful deal saver when, for example, your client needs to do a state housing loan that has a minimum middle credit score requirement of 620 and your client's score is 618. I have personally used this tactic many times with lots of success.

Back to your open house. Carlos and Nina are renting a home about six blocks away from your listing. They really want to stay in the neighborhood and think that this home would work well for their family. Nina explains that they have done well with their budget and savings, but she hasn't been able to convince Carlos that they need to establish a credit rating. Carlos insists that everything be paid for in cash. Because of this, Nina has assumed there's no point in applying for a mortgage.

Q. What if I don't have a credit history with the bureaus and no credit scores? Can I still get a mortgage?

A. Yes. A common loan program used for borrowers with no credit scores is FHA. It allows for "alternative" credit to be established by documenting utility payments, insurance premiums, rent, and other monthly payments not reported to a credit bureau. This documentation helps to establish a borrower's credit performance. When alternative credit is used the loan must be manually underwritten, as opposed to using underwriting software.

MAKING DOWN PAYMENTS

Brenda has stopped by your open house and is looking for a starter home as well. She hasn't been to see a lender yet and she's unsure of how much of her savings she should use for down payment.

Q. How much down payment is usually necessary when you are buying a primary residence?

A. If you have acceptable credit, income, and reserves, no down payment is necessary. If your credit has some rough spots, the presence of down payment can be a determining underwriting factor for an approved loan decision.

Q. Is my savings account the only acceptable source for a down payment?

A. No. Depending on the loan program, down payment can be gift funds from family, grant funds from special city or county programs, a withdrawal from a retirement account, or even a secured loan against an asset you own. (If you get a new loan, you must qualify with the new loan payment as well as your other debts.) It is not acceptable, under most programs, to use unsecured borrowed funds (a cash advance from a credit card) for down payment or to satisfy reserve requirements. Typically, any large deposits in your accounts will be scrutinized by an underwriter and proof of the source of those funds is required.

Q. How much down payment is smart?

A. Now here's the question that will trigger endless debates. This answer is the Tracey version. Sometimes the amount of down payment is dictated by the amount of mortgage you can qualify for. If the home sells for $250,000 and you can only qualify for a $200,000 mortgage, there's your answer. If your source of down payment is your savings (as opposed to money borrowed from a 401k), and it's adequate to cover a 20% down payment or more, that would be a great place to start. With a 20% down payment, you will avoid the requirement to pay mortgage insurance (the insurance premium required, and usually paid monthly with your payment, that protects the lender against default losses).

The next part of this answer is where a borrower has to analyze their own comfort level, saving habits, and probably consult a financial planner. In Brenda's case let's say a) she's a first-time homebuyer, and b) she has $10,000 in her savings. The home you're showcasing today has a sales price of $200,000.

My first rule is, *never* deplete your savings to buy a house if you can avoid it. (I'm saying this even though many of my first-time homebuyers purchase their homes with no money out-of-pocket, no money in the bank, and I send them off at closing with thanks and a little prayer. A savings account these days is a wonderful, but scarce commodity within the first-time homebuyer group.) Unless a borrower has a way of re-building that savings very quickly, it's always a huge risk to be without backup funds. Brenda has a great opportunity to have the best of both worlds. She can purchase a home and still have some financial stability that most first-time homebuyers don't enjoy.

Brenda will be surprised to know how little impact her $10,000 will have on her monthly payment. For every $1000 that Brenda puts down on her new home, she will reduce her monthly payment by approximately $6.32 (based on an interest rate of 6.5%). So best-case scenario, with her entire $10,000 down, she will save $63.20 per month. Most borrowers expect the impact to be at least triple that. Long term, over the life of a 30-year mortgage, the savings is more significant at $22,752.

In many cases, the difference between financial difficulty and financial crisis can be a savings account. Brenda's $10,000 savings seems like a lot of money to all of us until you put it into this perspective: She makes $5000 per month. Her net take-home income is $3700 after taxes, 401k deductions, etc. So $10,000 represents less than three months of net income. Experts recommend a reserve of six months of your income to be better prepared for setbacks.

In Brenda's case, she qualifies for her state's low-interest housing program. She can have a seller pay all of her closing costs and finance 100% of her home purchase, leaving her entire savings account intact. This would be my advice for a great combination of home ownership and some peace of mind.

Other clients who have the savings but not the luxury of a great credit history may have to put the entire balance of their savings into the loan to make it work. At this point they have to evaluate their priorities and how much risk they are willing to take.

LIQUID RESERVES

Your next lookers (at this open house that is going very well so far) are Wes and Kelly. They are walking dreamily from room to room lamenting about how they wish they were "ready" to buy. Without trying to appear too nosy, you talk with them about what "ready" means. You find out that Kelly's dad has warned them that there is no point in talking with a lender until they have at least six months' worth of house payment saved in the bank. Her dad said they call them "reserves." They calculate that they will qualify for about a $1500 house payment so they are working on saving $9000, or six months' reserves.

Q. What are liquid reserves?

A. Funds that are either in the form of "cash-in-hand" like money in the bank or funds that can easily be converted into cash, like a mutual fund. Seventy percent of 401k or retirement savings funds are considered liquid if the funds are fully vested. We only count 70% of the funds because we are allowing for the tax penalty that will occur if the funds are withdrawn.

Q. How much reserve do we really need to qualify?

A. Dad's theory about reserves is a little off. While having $9000 in the bank is a great idea from a financial stability standpoint, it's not, in many cases, required for loan qualifying. When purchasing a single-family primary residence using a 30-year fixed loan, which is a lower risk loan purpose, property type, and loan product, a borrower may qualify with no reserves at all. The key here is usually that the borrower has excellent credit. Another borrower trying to do the exact same loan may need one to six months of reserves in order to qualify because of lower credit scores.

Automated underwriting can be a wonderful tool for telling borrowers exactly what they need to do in order to get approved. Because the influence of reserves can be so powerful in the underwriting process, there are many times when a borrower cannot be approved today, but can be offered the scenario where approval is possible.

Loan officers can simply increase the amount of reserves

on the application and run the loan through the underwriting software again for a new recommendation. We can then let a borrower know that once they have a certain amount of savings documented in their account, their loan will be pre-approved.

The higher the risk, the more reserves required. Kelly's dad had recently purchased a three-unit property as an investment. It was the first mortgage loan he'd done in 20 years. His loan officer had explained that he would need six months of reserve in order to qualify for this mortgage. He didn't understand that this requirement varies with loan risk. He assumed that it was a standard condition.

DEBT-TO-INCOME RATIO

As your day goes on, Candice comes in just to take a look around. She, like your previous lookers, isn't quite ready to purchase yet. She has done some calculations and thinks that her debt-to-income ratio is too high, but she's not sure she's calculated it right. But she is excited because she only has three more $300 car payments to make and her car will be paid off. After it's paid off, she'll go see a lender.

Q. How is a debt-to-income ratio calculated?

A. There are two debt-to-income ratios that are important to underwriting a loan. The first compares the housing debt (the proposed new monthly house payment) to the total gross (before taxes and deductions) income. This is the housing ratio. The second compares the total debt, including the new house payment, to the total gross income. This is the total debt-to-income ratio. Candice makes $5300 per month. The proposed house payment on this home with a state housing finance loan is $1570.

Housing ratio: $1570 ÷ $5300 = 29.62%

Candice has $600 in regular monthly payments in addition to her $300 car payment. If we add $1570 + $600 + $300 = $2470 we get her total proposed debt with her car payment.

Total debt-to-income ratio: $2470 ÷ $5300 = 46.6%

Without her car payment, her ratio becomes:

Revised total debt-to-income ratio:
$2170 ÷ $5300 = 40.94%

Q. What is an acceptable ratio?
A. This is another big "it depends" answer. The standard underwriting rule of thumb says that a 30% housing ratio and a 42% total debt ratio is acceptable. This varies from loan program to loan program, and can be all over the board when you start using an automated underwriting program. Secondary factors such as credit score, reserves, and down payment play a huge part in determining a final "acceptable" ratio.

As a loan officer, I always counsel my clients with the following warning: Just because you can doesn't mean you should. It is so important to make sure that a buyer doesn't end up in a home that they really can't afford. Because of initiatives to better serve the low-to-moderate income borrowers, I have seen some pretty scary approved ratios lately. While that's great for you and me today, it's bad for business down the road if we've buried our client in a house they can't pay for. Not to mention, the disservice you've done your client and the heartache you've caused.

Q. Do I really have to wait until my car is paid off to go see a lender?

A. No. Installment debt that will be paid off in less than 10 months can be disregarded for the purposes of ratio calculations. Underwriters do have the discretionary power to override this rule if they feel that the monthly debt is too large and could become a hindrance on the borrower's ability to make the payment during those first months.

BUYING RENTAL PROPERTY

Tom, a past client whom you helped find a home a few blocks away last year, has stopped by your open house to say hello and ask a few questions. He is considering purchasing an investment property and isn't quite sure how to proceed.

Q. What kind of down payment will I need to have to purchase a rental property?

A. A minimum of 10% is standard on a one- to two-unit property. As of this writing, there may be a few 5% down programs out there, but the zero-down programs have been squelched. Defaults are on the rise as the country experiences a housing downturn and so many people jumped on the speculation band wagon too late. Three- or four-unit properties are higher risk and therefore require more down payment, usually at least 20%.

Q. How much of the projected rental income can I use to help me qualify?

A. On conventional loans, rental income can only be considered if the borrower has a two-year history of owning and managing a rental property. This track record is usually established by reviewing the borrower's past two years' tax returns. Schedule E will indicate properties owned and show rents received.

If a borrower has a two-year history, then 75% of projected rental income on the new property can be used to offset the new house payment. If not, the borrower must qualify with all of his current debt plus the new payment on the rental.

Because the two-year rule makes it tougher to purchase that first rental property, let Tom know that there is another approach to acquiring properties that can work well for some people. Tom could rent out his existing home as long as he's lived in it for at least one year and there are no restrictions on his loan regarding renting the property. (We don't want to get Tom into trouble with his lender or have him committing loan fraud.) Once Tom has a lease on his existing home, he can then purchase a new primary residence, possibly with 100% financing. Underwriting rules for primary purchase loans allow 75% of the projected income from the lease on his current home to be used to offset that home's payment.

While this scenario isn't perfect because Tom will have to move into the new property and use it as his primary residence for at least one year, it can be a way to achieve his goal of owning multiple properties without needing a large down payment.

Note: If a home is sold and hasn't been used as a primary residence for two of the last five years, there could be capital gains tax issues to deal with. Advise Tom to seek professional tax advice as he develops his property acquisition and potential sale strategy.

WHAT DOCUMENTS ARE NEEDED?

Your day is just about to wind up when another couple comes through the door. Ben and Bridget were referred to you by Tom. They know Tom because he lives next door to Ben's parents whom Ben and Bridget just moved in with. They noticed your sign and decided to stop in, since they hadn't gotten around to calling you yet. This couple is really doing their research and like all thorough buyers, they have a million questions. Once they get through the property, neighborhood, and price inquiries they move on to the loan stuff.

Q. We are getting ready to go see a lender but all of our financial documents are boxed up since we just moved into my parents' basement. Can you tell us what documents the lender will want so we know what to dig out of the boxes?

A. Here's what you will need:

- Last two pay stubs

- Last two years' W2s

- Last two years' federal tax returns (if self-employed, commissioned, or have other income sources that can be documented through the return)

- Last two months' bank statements

- Most recent 401k/retirement/other investment statements

- Driver's license

- Social security card

- Divorce decrees and bankruptcy papers

- Proof of other income sources (social security, disability, trust income, etc.)

Q. Why do they need my social security card?

A. Lenders are required to validate social security numbers. Applicants are required to present acceptable documentation to assist with this process. A social security card is the most common form of documentation. If a social security card is not available, W2 forms are the next most common form of documentation used.

Q. Why do they need my driver's license?

A. Lenders are subject to compliance with the Patriot Act. We must establish our borrower's identity and document the file.

MAKING EXTRA MORTGAGE PAYMENTS

You have found just the right house for Sam and Julie in the neighborhood they wanted. They've lined up financing and are waiting for the closing, so everything's good to go. As they're preparing for the closing, they ask you another one of those questions you'll get all the time for which it's good to have a ready answer.

Q. After we buy our home, is it smart to pay extra money toward principal every month?

A. Every couple should analyze their own circumstances and seek the advice of a financial planner, but here is the Tracey version of the answer: It depends. (Big surprise, huh?) While paying extra toward principal over the life of a mortgage loan can result in significant savings—as can paying off the loan early—it is way down the priority list of things to do with extra monthly income.

I always advise clients to take a hard look at their savings, retirement planning, credit card balances, and kids' college funds. If all of those items are adequately funded (or paid off) and you still have money burning a hole in your pocket, wonderful! You are the exception to the rule. Paying additional principal on your mortgage can save you thousands upon thousands of dollars over the life of a loan. Go for it.

Q. What about bi-weekly payments?
A. Bi-weekly payments serve three purposes:

1. Your payment is made in smaller amounts every two weeks.
2. You will end up making one extra monthly payment every year.
3. If you keep this mortgage, you will pay it off early.

Many borrowers love this option because they feel like the smaller payments are easier to make. They also tend to lack the discipline to pay extra principal on their own, so this forces them into the practice.

I'm not a fan of the bi-weekly payment option because you have to pay setup fees and you could accomplish the same thing on your own by simply paying 1/12 of a mortgage payment extra each month with your regular monthly payment. As I stated before, I'm also in favor of using the extra money many other places before I'd pay down the mortgage.

LAST WORD

Nobody has to tell you that while a home purchase is usually the largest financial decision a person will make, it is still a highly emotional decision. Some people assume it would be all about the numbers, but all seasoned real estate professionals know that's not true. Homeownership is more ego than economics. It's a giant gold star that says, "I am worthy."

But to get the gold star, the client has to get past the loan officer, and we are scary. I've always said we might as well greet our clients at the door, hand them a hospital gown, tell them to get undressed, and we'll be with them in a minute. Financial exposure is so not fun.

This is where you come in. Part of this emotional play are the relationships you build with every conversation you have. Saving a deal, or making one happen, can be all about having the right information at the right time for the right prospective client. Your ability to offer encouragement and knowledge can be the little boost of confidence that a buyer needed to make the next step or to decide that you are the Realtor for them!

CHAPTER 14

What You Should Know About Homeowners' Associations

Homeowners' Associations (HOAs) are not just for condos any-more. They are everywhere and that trend will continue. Here in Utah, it is rare to see a subdivision of single-family homes created that does not have an HOA. The legal descriptions vary from Planned Unit Development (PUD) to Cluster Subdivision and the amenities offered by each will vary as well. There can be everything from a few thousand square feet of open public space, to elaborate clubhouses with pools, tennis courts, walking trails, and parks.

I'm headed for my soapbox now, so beware.

The huge surge in the number of HOAs is also being accompanied by another huge surge: more and more litigation. This is the party that I don't want you invited to. The majority of problems tend to be between the owners themselves and the HOA or the project developer. However, lack of understanding regarding HOAs, how they work (or don't work in some cases), and how a lender reviews a project to determine if it's compliant with underwriting rules can really put you, the Realtor, up the creek without a paddle pretty quickly.

Let's try to get a basic handle on HOAs first. (Keep in mind that this is a general and broad overview and will vary from state to state and community to community.)

HOA BASICS

An HOA, if incorporated, is created under a state's nonprofit corporation act, as well as its specific state statutes that govern condominiums and PUDs. It should be organized with the following governing documents:

- Articles of Incorporation

- Bylaws

- Declarations or Covenants, Conditions, and Restrictions (CC&Rs)

There should also be officially adopted Rules and Regulations. While these are not part of the governing documents, they are extremely important to an owner and enforceable by the HOA.

Each document has specific purposes and may cover the following:

Articles of Incorporation

- Declares the purposes of the organization.

- Explains membership.

- Describes land use.

- Provides for Board of Trustees.

- Provides for assessments.

- Establishes meetings and provisions for amendment.

Bylaws

- Administration and procedures of corporation

- Details on meetings, voting procedures, board selection, committees, assessments, amendments, and fines

Covenants, Conditions, and Restrictions

- Restrictions regarding common and private property

- Established to preserve property values and maintain a pleasant living environment

- Details on dwelling setbacks, fences, colors, architecture, etc.

Rules and Regulations

- Clarifies governing documents or issues not addressed in documents.

- Created solely by the board and not voted on by membership.

Most larger HOAs that require monthly payment of fees (some HOAs have annual billing) will employ management companies to handle billing and fee collections, as well as other administrative duties. This is a great service and a good management company can be instrumental in keeping things running well.

A well-organized HOA is a fantastic asset to its community. The difficulty in achieving this goal can be great, however. HOAs are like complex little municipal governments. There is a lot involved in running one and keeping it protected legally through proper documentation and procedures. Now top this off with the fact that your board is comprised of all volunteers, most with well-meaning intentions, but not always the time or expertise to handle the various issues that present themselves. You can see where the problems begin to crop up.

It's imperative that a board have the necessary procedures and authority in place to enforce its documents and rules. Enforcement consistency makes for happy neighbors and less conflict. So how does a board enforce policies on behalf of the membership?

These are examples of the authority that should (in most

cases) be granted to a board in order to maintain the HOA's policies:

- Provide informal hearings for conflicts between lot owners.

- Impose fines from a pre-determined fine schedule.

- Deny access to common use areas.

- Shut off utilities (if the HOA "owns" the service, i.e., a private water system).

- Correct violations and charge owner with costs and fines.

- File liens for nonpayment of assessments.

- Initiate foreclosure for nonpayment of assessments.

WHAT YOU CAN DO

Why am I telling you all this? Because when you are helping a buyer find a home, the HOA of which your buyer will be a member will play a large part in his or her future happiness. A poorly run or disorganized HOA could result in one or more of the following problems:

- Large, unexpected increases in assessments or special assessments for large maintenance projects that weren't included in the budget

- Constant unresolved conflicts with neighbors

- Poor or no maintenance of common facilities

By asking for all of the HOA's documents and reviewing them with your client you can help them make a more informed choice. If the current owners don't have a copy for your review, the board should be able to provide one. You can always get a copy from the county as these documents should be recorded against the property.

This brings me to another subject: notice. Should you decide not to review these documents with your client and a problem arises later, your client will still be subject to these documents whether they reviewed them or not. The buyer is considered to have "notice" of these rules and restrictions because they are recorded against the property and are a matter of public record.

So AJ and Sophia love the house you've found them in a PUD. It has a great yard and will be perfect once they add a cute shed back in the corner to store their lawn mower and garden tools. Two months later you get a phone call from an unhappy AJ who has just received a letter from his HOA that the cute shed he spent $700 on at Home Depot must be removed immediately. Apparently the CC&Rs don't allow sheds. Now he wants to know who is going to reimburse him for the shed. He says he wouldn't have purchased the property in the first place if he had known this.

At this point, telling him that there's nothing you can do, because proper legal notice has been satisfied by the recording of the covenants against his property, is not going to go over too well. Nor is telling him it was his responsibility to ask for these documents. He's pretty sure that was your job as his agent.

While you may have no liability here, what you do have is a frustrated customer who wants some answers. Don't put yourself in this position! It's guaranteed: 99% of your clients would never think to review the governing documents affecting a property they are about to purchase. Protect them and yourself. Help them do the research!

Two other items for possible review are the HOA's financial report and minutes from homeowners' meetings for the last year. These can be a window on conflicts, problems, and potential future problems.

To complicate the situation even further, mortgage lenders have specific criteria that an existing project must meet in order to approve a loan on a condominium or property in a PUD. (Detached properties in condominium projects or PUDs don't have to be reviewed for compliance with the issues below.) As a selling or buying agent, you will want to get the answers to these questions, preferably before the lender does, so that you know what you are getting into.

- Is the HOA involved in a lawsuit? This could be an expensive problem for an HOA even if the outcome is good, and it could prohibit a loan from being approved.

- Does the HOA have any planned special assessments? If our borrower's HOA fees are going up, the lender wants to approve the loan with the new higher amount, not to mention you've got disclosure issues as an agent. (This is my personal opinion, not legal fact.)

- Does any one entity own more than 10% of the units? This can be a problem for smaller condo projects. Lenders are a stickler about this 10% rule and it can make financing a property very difficult. This can be really maddening for a seller who, at the time they purchased, had no problem with financing because the answer to this question used to be no. Now, because of the actions of other property owners, their property is harder to sell.

- What percentage of the units is currently being rented? How many units total? How many are rented out? Another big deal for lenders. They want to see that the units are predominately owner-occupied. High rental percentages have been tied to declining property values and defaults. The reason the second part of this question is so vital is so that you can get an indication if a project has a rental percentage that is creeping too close to the 60% mark (conventional loan limitation) or 51% mark (FHA limit). Why would you want to put your buyers into a property that could present problems for them later on when they try to sell? Hopefully, you'll be the agent helping them sell it and wouldn't you rather be selling a great property with a healthy HOA?

Educating your client on HOA living and helping them research a property will be well worth your time. Informed clients are happy clients and happy clients come back.

CHAPTER 15

Home Inspections: Preventive Measures

"The home inspector killed my deal." I've heard this comment more than a few times from Realtors. I'm sure, in some cases, this is true—either because an inspector was incompetent, or overzealous in his attempt to provide his services and justify his inspection fee. Unfortunately, it's usually the condition of the house itself that killed the deal.

This is another reality of your career that you can embrace and understand, or go back to the corner, cross your fingers, and hope it all works out. Let's assume you want to go with Plan A.

I realize that there may be nothing wrong with your attitude toward home inspections. It's the seller who ultimately sets the tone on this subject. When someone is selling a home, they are usually less than enthusiastic about spending a bunch of time doing improvements or repairs on a home they are leaving. This is frustrating for you because an uncooperative seller makes your job even more difficult. I can hear many of you now saying, "Repairs?! I'd be happy at this point if some of my sellers would just vacuum occasionally!"

Home inspections, if they aren't already customary in your market, are becoming a common standard practice in many areas that rarely used them ten years ago. The Department of Housing and Urban Development actively advocates the use of a professional home inspector to homebuyers. Many Realtors use them as a marketing tool when they list a home, offering to pay for a home inspection upon listing to provide the sellers with valuable property condition information. The seller can then correct conditions to improve the property's market appeal.

Choosing a home inspector can be difficult since this is a highly unregulated industry. Be sure to use a company/individual that offers:

- Certification with 5 + years in the inspection business, preferably with a strong construction trade or engineering background

- Membership in a national professional trade organization. American Society of Home Inspectors (ASHI) or National Association of Certified Home Inspectors (NACHI) are the two most common

- Client participation during inspection (this process should be about education)

- A thorough written report that complies with ASHI or NACHI standards

- Additional testing and evaluation services such as radon, mold, methamphetamine, and air quality

If a seller prefers not to have a home inspection performed at the time they list the home, there is plenty that they can do on their own to get their home in tip-top showing shape:

- Inspect the roof. Replace any missing or deteriorated shingles and repair any leaks.

- Inspect the foundation for major cracks. If found, a structural engineer may be needed to determine cause and remedy.

- Check basement and/or crawlspace for water/excess moisture.

- Have heating and air conditioning systems checked by a licensed professional.

- Check for broken/missing outlet covers, light bulbs, and light fixtures.

- Replace dirty filters in heating and ventilation system.

- Have chimneys professionally inspected and cleaned.

- Trim trees and shrubs. Contact your local utility company to trim any trees near power lines.

- Apply new caulk and weather stripping around windows and doors.

- Clean debris from gutters, repair broken gutters and extensions to ensure proper drainage away from home.

- Replace bathroom caulk/grout where necessary to prevent leaks and improve appearance.

- Repair leaky faucets.

- Tighten door knobs.

- Replace damaged screens.

- Replace broken panes of glass.

- Secure loose railings.

- Patch small holes in walls and ceilings and repaint.

- Test smoke detectors and replace batteries.

- Test carbon monoxide detectors, or install one if none is present.

- Test all GFI outlets.

- Check that electrical wiring under sink to garbage disposal is protected in conduit.

- Repair holes or missing sheetrock on garage firewall (wall next to house).

- If furnace and hot water tank are in the garage, verify that they are on a platform 18 inches above the floor and located in an area where a car won't run into them.

- Tighten loose toilets.

- Repair constantly running toilets.

- Check for water leaks under all sinks.

- Have septic tank pumped if it's been over five years since previous service.

This list will address the most common problems that home inspectors find in homes. Should your client detect any substance that appears to be mold (and the affected area is less than ten square feet), they should first remedy the source of the moisture that's causing the growth and then proceed with careful cleanup. (Guidelines for safe cleanup and other mold information can be found at www.moldtips.com.) Larger areas of mold growth may require professional removal services.

I've talked previously about the emotional side to your business, and this property condition issue can spark some pretty defensive reactions. I sold my home last year and I can tell you that all logic was thrown out the window when the buyer started asking questions about some minor items that the home inspector had mentioned in his report. I immediately had two simultaneous thoughts: "Are you saying my home isn't good enough?" and "This home is 30 years old. Deal with it." Aaaaaaaaahhhhhhh! What was I thinking? This buyer just wanted some simple answers. She was spending a lot of money and had every right to question these items. Bless the Realtor who put up with me!

CHAPTER 16

Appraisals and Sale Prices: Pulling It Together

Is there anybody in the real estate business who has not had headaches over an appraisal? And some of the biggest headaches are suffered by the appraisers themselves. Trust me. Appraisers are not happy to come in with a value lower than the contract price. They want to be loved, too. They want repeat business. They want happy customers.

The sub-prime and niche lending market woes, along with the general slide in the housing industry across the country, is making it an unpleasant time to be an appraiser. Mortgage fraud is at an all-time high as well, and most fraud schemes won't work without an appraiser willing to play along. This has put lenders on the warpath when it comes to appraisal scrutiny. Scrutiny can come in three forms: (1) an underwriting review during loan approval, (2) an appraisal review, or (3) a review appraisal.

This puts a lot more pressure on you, the listing agent, to determine an appropriate sales price for a home and then convince the owner to list at that price. So many sellers want to "construct" a sales price by figuring out how much profit they want to make and then adding their loan payoffs, closing costs, and your commission. This is understandable but not practical.

1. *Underwriting Review.* An underwriting review, in the best circumstances, is done by an experienced, local underwriter who is very familiar with the area they are approving loans in. They understand the subtleties of location, trends, and property use. In other words, they have a good "feel" for their market. This type of review is always part of the loan underwriting process.

An underwriter will examine the appraisal for accuracy regarding the address, transaction type, and contract details so that typographical errors can be fixed. She will compare it to the loan application, title report, and contract. She will study the comparables for suitability and review the adjustments made to each comparable. If she is not comfortable with the appraisal she may ask for additional comparables to be added, or she can ultimately adjust the value downward.

In rare instances of obvious incompetence by the appraiser, she can require a new appraisal. This will happen almost exclusively with conventional lending. FHA and VA appraisals are assigned case numbers and the appraisal "follows" the property for six months. While "challenging" the FHA or VA appraisal is allowed, replacing it is usually not.

2. *Appraisal Review.* An appraisal review is where an appraisal must be reviewed by a second appraiser in order to corroborate the value. This is very common in the niche loan market (stated income and no income verification loans). The lender chooses the appraiser who will perform the review from a list of approved providers.

This appraiser will review the appraisal, just as an underwriter would, with extra emphasis on the comparable sales. He will actually verify the comp information with the multiple listing service (MLS) it was pulled from, or whatever other data source the original appraiser used. He will look at all other sales in the area to determine if the comps used were the most appropriate. He will also look for any previous sales data on the subject property and make sure that it was disclosed properly.

3. *Review Appraisal.* A review appraisal is when a complete second appraisal is done to substantiate the value on the first appraisal. Again, this is a common requirement in the niche marketplace and in situations where the loan amounts are higher. The lender chooses the review appraiser from their approved list.

Typically, any loan for $1,000,000 or more requires two appraisals be included in the initial loan file for underwriting. They are done simultaneously by two different appraisers and both appraisals are part of the permanent loan file.

Many lenders are starting to require two appraisals on loan amounts for $650,000 or higher.

Appraisal reviews and review appraisals look for information accuracy and compliance with the Uniform Standards of Professional Appraisal Practice (USPAP). The most common problem I've seen with review processes has to do with the comparable sales data that the appraiser used to arrive at the value.

COMPARABLE SALES DATA

Comparable sales, or comps, are homes that have sold (preferably within the last six months) within the same neighborhood that have similar attributes as the subject property. If possible, the comps should be similar in style, age, and size. An appraisal will have at least three comps but may contain as many as six, depending on available data. Sometimes lack of data within the immediate neighborhood will force the appraiser to go outside the area for comps. Once an appraiser goes outside of the area, he will need to make his value case even stronger and additional comps can help. Often comps used in addition to the standard three will be homes that are "under contract" but not yet sold. While they can't be used as "core data," they can help to strengthen the appraiser's final number.

Another hair-pulling event that happens in a quickly appreciating market is called "data delay." This is when prices are going up so quickly that the closed sales data doesn't always support your contract sales price. We had a crazy market here in Utah during 2005 and 2006. Phone calls were flying from one Realtor to another begging them to immediately update the MLS as soon as a property closed so that the comp would be available for use. I've even had people delay their settlement so that another sale could close and the comp for that sale could be used on the appraisal so there wouldn't be a value problem.

Quickly appreciating seller's markets also produce a higher number of for sale by owner (FSBO) sales. It's easy to sell and sellers think they are saving a lot of money by not paying commission. (You and I know differently, but that's another subject for another day.) This is especially problematic in a nondisclosure state for purposes of gathering comp information. (Yes, there are states out there, and Utah is one of them, that do not disclose sales price information on deeds. In Utah, all of our property is sold for $10 according to public record.) So I see Realtors pounding on doors and making phone calls to FSBOs to see if they'll release their HUD1 settlement statements for use by an appraiser. Many nondisclosure states also don't have a transfer tax, which means that you can't "back in" to a sales price. While the Mortgage or Trust Deed is a matter of public record, it isn't much help.

Conversely, a rapidly declining market usually has fewer comps due to a sales slowdown, but the prices tend to be higher from the previous months. The dilemma here is that even though your comparable sales prices look great, a) the appraiser has to note that the market is declining, and b) underwriters are obligated under lender guidelines to adjust appraisal values down depending on how rapidly the values are headed lower. This is definitely not a fun market to be operating in.

OTHER FACTORS THAT CAN AFFECT VALUE

Sales concessions can also create a predicament on an appraisal value. It is so important that you understand the acceptable sales concession limits for your buyer's loan program before you write an offer. Concession limits differ based on loan program and loan-to-value percentages. They can be anywhere from 2% to 9%. If you have sales concessions that exceed the acceptable limit, the underwriter has to reduce the appraised value by the amount of concession excess.

It's also vital not to include personal property or items not customarily included in the sales price of the home. It will ultimately result in a deduction from the appraised value. This is not a big deal if a home appraises higher than the sales price, but we all know that's the exception and not the rule. An addendum to the contract can disclose the property or items being sold stating they are to be conveyed on a separate bill of sale and are not included in the sale price.

WHEN THE APPRAISAL IS LOW

Determining a fair market value is easier said than done, I know, but sellers feel personally insulted when their home won't appraise at their perceived value. Avoid the hurt feel-ings, if possible, and list the home with the right price from the start. If you do your best, and the appraisal still comes in low, what is your next move?

1. *Never call the appraiser (unless you ordered the appraisal).* Typically, an appraisal is being done for the purposes of the mortgage loan and the lender is the appraiser's client, not you. He has absolutely no obligation to discuss this appraisal with you.

2. *Determine whether the low appraisal even matters.* In come cases, a low value does not affect the loan. This is true in cases where the client has a large down payment. I had a loan where data delay caused this very problem. We explained the issue to the borrower and they were comfortable proceeding with the current sales price.

3. *Provide the lender with the data you used to price the home or any other comps you feel are appropriate.* Appraisers are happy and willing to incorporate any viable comps that you can provide as long as the use of that comp conforms to appraisal standards. Remember, it's not the appraiser's job to get the value we want; it's his job to provide a value opinion based on the readily available data. Maybe you know of a closing in the neighborhood that will help. Call the Realtor and ask them to update the MLS right away. Knock on FSBO doors, or have your client go to their FSBO neighbor and ask to use their home as a comp (if you are in a nondisclosure state). While an appraiser in a nondisclosure state is happy

to use FSBO data, it is not their job to knock on doors to get it.

4. **Drop the sales price to match the appraised value.** This option may not be too painful if the value difference is small and your sellers are flexible. Sometimes "sweetening the pot" with a commission reduction to make the sale work will convince a seller to go forward. None of us like dropping our profit margin to save a deal, but sometimes it's what we have to do to get to the settlement table.

5. **Do not expect a request for a second appraisal to be granted.** FHA and VA appraisers allow challenges and will review any new data that is presented but getting a new one is not an option (without involving a regional HUD or VA office and proving complete incompetence). There would also have to be complete lack of the confidence in the appraiser's ability before an underwriter would allow a second appraisal to be considered on a conventional loan. Loan officers who simply order a new appraisal because they didn't like the first one, and don't disclose the existence of the first appraisal to the underwriter, have committed loan fraud. It's that simple.

I'll keep my fingers crossed that appraisal problems don't plague too many of your deals. But look at the bright side: It could be worse. It could be the 70's when the only lending game in town was your bank or savings and loan.

They had their own appraisers and the only comps they had and were allowed to use was their own in-house data. Data was defined as a card file system with a picture stapled to it. There was no MLS, no email, no PDF files, and a speedy closing was 90 days. No thanks.

APPENDIX A

State Housing Agency Information

Alabama Housing Finance Authority
www.ahfa.com

Alaska Housing Finance Corporation
www.ahfc.state.ak.us

Arizona Department of Housing/Arizona Housing Finance
  Authority
www.housingaz.com

Arkansas Development Finance Authority
www.state.ar.us/adfa

California Housing Finance Agency
www.calhfa.ca.gov

Colorado Housing and Finance Authority
www.colohfa.org

Connecticut Housing Finance Authority
www.chfa.org

Delaware State Housing Authority
www.destatehousing.com

District of Columbia Housing Finance Agency
www.dchfa.org

Florida Housing Finance Corporation
www.floridahousing.org

Georgia Department of Community Affairs/Georgia
    Housing and Finance Authority
www.dca.state.ga.us

Hawaii Housing Finance and Development Corporation
www.hawaii.gov/dbedt/hhfdc

Idaho Housing and Finance Association
www.ihfa.org

Illinois Housing Development Authority
www.ihda.org

Indiana Housing and Community Development Authority
www.in.gov/ihfa

Iowa Finance Authority
www.IowaFinanceAuthority.gov

Kansas Housing Resources Corporation
www.kshousingcorp.org

Kentucky Housing Corporation
www.kyhousing.org

Louisiana Housing Finance Authority
www.lhfa.state.la.us

MaineHousing
www.mainehousing.org

Maryland Department of Housing and Community
　Development
www.dhcd.state.md.us

MassHousing
www.masshousing.com

Michigan State Housing Development Authority
www.michigan.gov/mshda

Minnesota Housing
www.mhfa.state.mn.us

Mississippi Home Corporation
www.mshomecorp.com

Missouri Housing Development Commission
www.mhdc.com

Montana Board of Housing/Housing Division
www.housing.mt.gov

Nebraska Investment Finance Authority
www.nifa.org

Nevada Housing Division
www.nvhousing.state.nv.us

New Hampshire Housing Finance Authority
www.nhhfa.org

New Jersey Housing and Mortgage Finance Agency
www.nj-hmfa.com

New Mexico Mortgage Finance Authority
www.housingnm.org

New York State Housing Finance Agency/State of New York
   Mortgage Agency
www.nyhomes.org

North Carolina Housing Finance Agency
www.nchfa.com

North Dakota Housing Finance Agency
www.ndhfa.org

Ohio Housing Finance Agency
www.ohiohome.org

Oklahoma Housing Finance Agency
www.ohfa.org

Oregon Housing and Community Services
www.ohcs.oregon.gov

Pennsylvania Housing Finance Agency
www.phfa.org

Puerto Rico Housing Finance Authority
www.gdp-pur.com

Rhode Island Housing
www.rihousing.com

South Carolina State Housing Finance and Development
    Authority
www.schousing.com

South Dakota Housing Development Authority
www.sdhda.org

Tennessee Housing Development Agency
www.tennessee.gov/thda

Texas Department of Housing and Community Affairs
www.tdhca.state.tx.us

Utah Housing Corporation
www.utahhousingcorp.org

Vermont Housing Finance Agency
www.vhfa.org

Virgin Islands Housing Finance Authority
www.vihfa.gov

Virginia Housing Development Authority
www.vhda.com

Washington State Housing Finance Commission
www.wshfc.org

West Virginia Housing Development Fund
www.wvhdf.com

Wisconsin Housing and Economic Development Authority
www.wheda.com

Wyoming Community Development Authority
www.wyomingcda.com

APPENDIX B

Home Listing Checklist

☐ Who owns this home? (check county records)
☐ Are all owners available to sign listing and closing documents?
☐ If owned by entity:
    ☐ Is entity in good standing?
    ☐ Get copy of organization documents for title company
    ☐ Who can sign to convey real estate?
    ☐ Are all required signers available to sign listing and closing documents?
☐ Has home been previously listed in the last three years?

- [ ] Previous sales price?
- [ ] Reason for listing withdrawal?
- [ ] How long has seller owned home?
- [ ] Has seller filed Chapter 7 or Chapter 13 bankruptcy?
- [ ] Net sheet?
- [ ] Are sellers aware of any unpaid judgments, property taxes, or child support?
- [ ] Termite inspection?
- [ ] Septic inspection?
- [ ] Water test?
- [ ] Is home price within FHA/state housing limits?
- [ ] Flood zone?
- [ ] Preview home condition
- [ ] Home Owners Association?
  - [ ] Contact information for board and management company, if applicable
  - [ ] Get all governing documents
  - [ ] Get financial statement and homeowners' meeting minutes
- [ ] Review logistics with sellers
  - [ ] Contract deadlines
  - [ ] Settlement
  - [ ] Closing
  - [ ] Funding
  - [ ] Recording
  - [ ] Actual move-out date / key surrender
  - [ ] Funds from sale / When does seller get their money?

C

Homebuyer/Offer Checklist

- [ ] Is buyer currently involved in Chapter 7 or Chapter 13 bankruptcy? (Buyer may not qualify for loan or may need permission to proceed from trustee.)
- [ ] Pre-approval letter?
- [ ] VA buyer?
  - [ ] Have they applied for Certificate of Eligibility?
  - [ ] If two borrowers, are they married or do both have VA entitlement?
- [ ] Are all buyers going to be in town for settlement?
  - [ ] If not, arrange for power-of-attorney and Alive and Well Letter if VA

- [ ] Is offer on property with Homeowners' Association?
  - [ ] Get HOA documents
  - [ ] HOA financial statements
  - [ ] Minutes from previous homeowners' meetings
  - [ ] Contact information for board and management company if applicable
- [ ] Review logistics with buyer
  - [ ] Contract deadlines
  - [ ] Settlement
  - [ ] Closing
  - [ ] Funding
  - [ ] Recording
  - [ ] Possession (keys)
  - [ ] When necessary funds for closing must be paid and what fund forms are acceptable (wires, cashiers checks, etc.)
- [ ] Review vesting on Warranty Deed at settlement

APPENDIX D

Flood Zones Defined

MODERATE- TO LOW-RISK AREAS

In communities that participate in the National Flood Insurance Program (NFIP), flood insurance is available to all property owners and renters with moderate to low risk. Insurance purchase is not required.

Zones B, C, and X

Areas outside the 1% annual chance floodplain; areas of 1% annual chance sheet flow flooding where average depths are less than one foot; areas of 1% annual chance stream flooding where the contributing drainage area is less than one square mile; or areas protected from the 1% annual chance flood by levees. No base flood elevations or depths are shown within this zone.

HIGH-RISK AREAS

In communities that participate in the NFIP, mandatory flood insurance purchase requirements apply to all A zones.

Zone A

Areas with 1% annual chance of flooding and a 26% chance of flooding over the life of a 30-year mortgage. Because detailed analyses are not performed for such areas, no depths or base flood elevations are shown within these zones.

Zone AE and A1–A30

Areas with a 1% annual chance of flooding and a 26% chance of flooding over the life of a 30-year mortgage. In most instances, base flood elevations derived from detailed analyses are shown at selected intervals within these zones.

Zone AH

Areas with a 1% annual chance of shallow flooding, usually in the form of a pond, with an average depth ranging from one to three feet. These areas have a 26% chance of flooding over the life of a 30-year mortgage. Base flood elevations derived from detailed analyses are shown at selected intervals within these zones.

Zone AO

River or stream flood hazard areas, and areas with a 1% or greater chance of shallow flooding each year, usually in the form of sheet flow, with an average depth ranging from one to three feet. These areas have a 26% chance of flooding over the life of a 30-year mortgage. Average flood depths derived from detailed analyses are shown within these zones.

Zone AR

Areas with a temporarily increased flood risk due to the building or restoration of a flood control system (such as a levee or a dam). Mandatory flood insurance purchase requirements will apply, but rates will not exceed the rates for unnumbered A zones if the structure is built or restored in compliance with Zone AR floodplain management regulations.

Zone A99

Areas with a 1% annual chance of flooding that will be protected by a federal flood control system where construction has reached specified legal requirements. No depths or base flood elevations are shown within these zones.

HIGH-RISK COASTAL AREAS

In communities that participate in the NFIP, mandatory flood insurance purchase requirements apply to all V zones.

Zone V

Coastal areas with a 1% or greater chance of flooding and an additional hazard associated with storm waves. These areas have a 26% chance of flooding over the life of a 30-year mortgage. No base flood elevations are shown within these zones.

Zone VE and V1–30

Coastal areas with a 1% or greater chance of flooding and an additional hazard associated with storm waves. These areas have a 26% chance of flooding over the life of a 30-year mortgage. Base flood elevations derived from detailed analyses are shown at selected intervals within these zones.

UNDETERMINED RISK AREAS

Undetermined risk areas are areas with possible but undetermined flood hazards.

Zone D

No flood hazard analysis has been conducted. Flood insurance rates are commensurate with the uncertainty of the flood risk.

Index

INDEX

Look for These Exciting Real Estate Titles at
www.amacombooks.org/go/realestate

A Survival Guide for Buying a Home by Sid Davis $17.95

A Survival Guide for Selling a Home by Sid Davis $15.00

Are You Dumb Enough to Be Rich? by G. William Barnett II $18.95

Everything You Need to Know Before Buying a Co-op, Condo, or Townhouse by Ken Roth $18.95

Make Millions Selling Real Estate by Jim Remley $18.95

Mortgages 101 by David Reed $16.95

Mortgage Confidential by David Reed $16.95

Real Estate Investing Made Simple by M. Anthony Carr $17.95

Real Estate Presentations That Make Millions by Jim Remley $18.95

The Complete Guide to Investing in Foreclosures by Steve Berges $17.95

The Consultative Real Estate Agent by Kelle Sparta $17.95

The First-Time Homeowner's Survival Guide by Sid Davis $16.00

The Home Buyer's Question and Answer Book by Bridget McCrea $16.95

The Landlord's Financial Tool Kit by Michael C. Thomsett $18.95

The Property Management Tool Kit by Mike Beirne $19.95

The Real Estate Agent's Business Planner by Bridget McCrea $19.95

The Real Estate Agent's Field Guide by Bridget McCrea $19.95

The Real Estate Agent's Guide to FSBOs by John Maloof $19.95

The Real Estate Investor's Pocket Calculator by Michael C. Thomsett $17.95

The Successful Landlord by Ken Roth $19.95

Who Says You Can't Buy a Home! by David Reed $17.95

Your Guide to VA Loans by David Reed $17.95

Your Successful Career as a Mortgage Broker by David Reed $18.95

Your Successful Real Estate Career, Fifth Edition by Kenneth W. Edwards $18.95

Available at your local bookstore, online, or call 800-250-5308.

Savings start at 40% on bulk orders of 5 copies or more!
Save up to 55%!
Prices are subject to change.
For details, contact AMACOM Special Sales
Phone: 212-903-8316   E-Mail: SpecialSls@amanet.org